Deuteronomy

God's Word for a New Generation

The secret things belong to the LORD our God, but the things that are revealed belong to us and to our children forever, that we may do all the words of this law.

Deuteronomy 29:29

By Gary Dunker

CONCORDIA PUBLISHING HOUSE · SAINT LOUIS

Copyright © 2008 Concordia Publishing House
3558 S. Jefferson Avenue
St. Louis, MO 63118-3968
1-800-325-3040 • www.cph.org

Written by Gary Dunker

Edited by Robert C. Baker

This publication may be available in braille, in large print, or on cassette tape for the visually impaired. Please allow 8 to 12 weeks for delivery. Write to Lutheran Blind Mission, 7550 Watson Road, St. Louis, MO 63119-4409; call toll-free 1-888-215-2455; or visit the Web site: www.blindmission.org.

1 2 3 4 5 6 7 8 9 10 13 12 11 10 09 08 07 06 05 04

Contents

Timeline....5
An Outline of Deuteronomy....6
Introduction....8
Lesson 1—A Turning Point....10
Lesson 2—You Belong to God....16
Lesson 3—Set Apart by God....22
Lesson 4—God's Moral Law....27
Lesson 5—Only by God's Righteousness....32
Lesson 6—New Tablets....38
Lesson 7—God's Ceremonial Law....44
Lesson 8—Celebrating God's Grace....50
Lesson 9—God's Civil Laws....56
Lesson 10—More Civil Laws....62
Lesson 11—Follow the Lord....67
Lesson 12—God's Covenant Ratified....73
Lesson 13—Succession of Leadership....79
Leader Notes
Preparing to Teach Deuteronomy....84
Lesson 1....89

Lesson 2 92
Lesson 3 95
Lesson 4 98
Lesson 5 101
Lesson 6 104
Lesson 7 107
Lesson 8 110
Lesson 9 113
Lesson 10 116
Lesson 11 118
Lesson 12 121
Lesson 13 124

History	*Date* (BC)	*Deuteronomy*
Joseph born *(Genesis 30:22–24)*	ca. **1915**	
Jacob settles in Egypt *(Genesis 46:5–7)*	**1876**	
Hammurabi begins reign in Babylonia	**1792**	
	1526	Moses born in Egypt *(Exodus 2:1–8)*
Amenhotep II becomes Pharaoh of Egypt	**1450**	
Exodus from Egypt	**1446**	*(Exodus 12:31–51)*
Hebrews wander in the wilderness	**1446–1406**	Moses writes Pentateuch *(Genesis–Deuteronomy)*
Construction of Tabernacle *(Exodus 25–30; 35–40)*	**1446**	
	1444	Moses and Aaron take census *(Numbers 1:1–46)*; send spies to Canaan *(Numbers 13:1–3; 28)*
Aaron dies on Mount Hor *(Numbers 33:38–39)*	**1406**	Moses dies on Mount Nebo *(Deuteronomy 34)*
Joshua leads Hebrews into Canaan; conquest begins *(Joshua 1–3)*	**1405**	
Joshua dies *(Joshua 24:29)*	**1399**	
Amenhotep IV "Akhenaton," father of Tutankhamen, becomes Pharaoh	**1352**	

An Outline of Deuteronomy

Israel's forty-year wait has ended. Out of a generation that rebelled against God, only three men remain: Moses, Joshua, and Caleb. Those who joined their voices with the spies returning from Canaan, saying, "We are not able to go up against the people, for they are stronger than we are" (Numbers 13:31), lie buried in the wilderness of Zin, southwest of the Dead Sea. The words they spoke were prophetic: "Would that we had died in the land of Egypt! Or would that we had died in this wilderness!" (Numbers 14:2). An entire generation's unbelief caused them to perish in the desert. Only their descendants and these three men remain.

While one generation gradually passed away, another was coming into maturity. Moses led this new generation from its encampment near Kadesh-barnea to the east side of the Jordan River. They had only heard about how their parents and grandparents had crossed the Red Sea. They themselves had not experienced God's guiding and guarding presence in the pillars of cloud and fire. Mount Sinai and God's holy laws were oral history for them. Now, by His grace, God will change all that—by affirming His Law and ratifying His covenant with them, a new generation.

Conservative Bible scholars point to Moses as the author of Deuteronomy as well as Genesis, Exodus, Leviticus, and Numbers. Deuteronomy itself confirms Moses as the author (1:1, 5; 31:9, 22, 24). In discussing marriage and divorce in the context of Deuteronomy 24 (see Matthew 19:3–8), Jesus affirmed Moses' authorship (see also Mark 12:19, 26 and John 5:45–47). Both Peter (Acts 3:22 and 7:37) and Paul did likewise (Romans 10:5, 19).

Scholars also note that Deuteronomy takes on the form of an ancient suzerain/vassal treaty, in which a powerful leader, called a suzerain, extended both his benevolence and his expectations to his vassals, the weaker party in the treaty. Traditionally, suzerain/vassal treaties included up to six sections: a preamble; a historical prologue; stipulations of the treaty; provisions for treaty renewal; a call upon witnesses to the treaty; and a list of blessings and curses.

The Scriptures use human language and grammar and contain historical narrative, poetry, and song. We should not be surprised, therefore, that the Holy Spirit would inspire Moses to use an ancient version of a legal document as an outline for his last book. The following outline takes note of that fact.

I. Preamble (1:1–1:5)
II. Historical Prologue (1:6–4:43)
III. Covenant Stipulations (4:44–26:19)
    A. Moral Law (4:44–11:32)
    B. Ceremonial Law (12:1–16:17)
    C. Civil Law (16:18–26:19)
IV. Covenant Ratification (27:1–30:20)
    A. Mount Ebal and Curses (27)
    B. Blessings and Curses (28)
    C. Covenant Renewal (29)
    D. The Blessings of Prosperity (30:1–10)
    E. The Offer of Life or Death (30:11–20)
V. Succession of Leadership (31:1–34:12)
    A. Joshua (31:1–13)
    B. Rebellion Foretold (31:14–19)
    C. Song of Moses (31:30–32:47)
    D. Last Days of Moses (32:48–34:12)

Introduction

The Old Testament Book of Deuteronomy concludes the Five Books of Moses, known collectively as the Pentateuch. In this book, God expresses His gracious intent in contract form, similar to an ancient Near Eastern suzerainty treaty. Just as people create contracts to express mutual pledges or agreements, God did likewise. Out of love, God bound Himself to His covenant people, promising His gracious and forgiving presence. In gratitude, His people promised to obey His moral, civil, and religious laws.

In Genesis, Moses' first book, we read how God selected Abraham to found a nation through whom He would bless the world with a Savior. In Exodus, we learn how God delivered this nation from bondage to a cruel oppressor, which points ahead to Christ and our deliverance from sin. Also in Exodus, we see how God established His covenant nation, spelling out the terms of His covenant, or agreement, at Mount Sinai. In Leviticus, we learn how God provided further regulations that allowed His people to enter His holy presence. In the Book of Numbers, we see how God remained faithful to His covenant, even though the faith of His chosen people and their obedience waned. As one generation died in rebellion, God raised up a second generation, bringing them to the edge of the Jordan River, across from the Promised Land. This is where Deuteronomy begins.

Deuteronomy received its title from Septuagint scholars. As these experts translated the Hebrew Old Testament into Greek, they applied the Greek *deuteronomion*, "a second law," to this book. However, Deuteronomy is not a second law, but a restatement of God's Word—both Law and Gospel—to a second generation. In Deuteronomy, Moses delivers a series of three farewell sermons: 1:1–4:43; 4:44–28:68; and chapters 29–33. In chapter 34, Joshua records Moses' death and burial.

When did Moses write Deuteronomy? King Solomon began building the temple in Jerusalem in the fourth year of his reign and 480 years after Israel left Egypt (1 Kings 6:1). Solomon's forty-year reign dates from 970–930 BC. The fourth year of his reign—966 BC—

allows us to date the exodus at 1446 BC. In Deuteronomy 1:3, we read, "In the fortieth year, on the first day of the eleventh month, Moses spoke to the people of Israel." This allows us date Deuteronomy at about 1406 BC.

Lesson 1

A Turning Point

God's people stared westward in wonder—across the Jordan River, into the land that God had promised to their ancestors. Long ago, God had promised the land they now strained to see to Abraham, their greatest patriarch (Genesis 15:7). God's people faithfully handed down this promise to succeeding generations: Abraham to Isaac, Isaac to Jacob, and Jacob to Joseph.

For a time, the Israelites had nearly forgotten God's promise, so Moses reminded them. He led them out of Egypt to their new home, a land God said was "flowing with milk and honey" (Exodus 3:8). They knew the story of how Moses had sent spies into the land. Now, as a new generation peers across the Jordan, they remember how ten spies had turned Israel's heart away from God. Only Moses, Joshua, and Caleb remained of the old generation. All of the rest of their ancestors—mothers and fathers, aunts and uncles, grandmothers and grandfathers—lie buried along the path that led them to the place where they now stood.

At times, the Israelites wavered in their faith, just as you and I often do. However, God remains faithful. Under Moses' leadership, He has brought the descendants of the exodus and wilderness crossing to the banks of the Jordan. The voice of Moses draws their attention. They turn to face him. They will listen to their remarkable leader, who himself is about to die. He will remind them of God's covenantal faithfulness that has and will continue to enable their willing obedience.

Ancient Suzerain/Vassal Treaties

Moses delivered a series of three sermons, which are recorded in the Bible's fifth book, Deuteronomy. Scholars have studied these sermons and have noted a similarity between their arrangement and ancient suzerain/vassal treaties. In ancient times, kings or rulers (suzerains) made treaties with lesser rulers (vassals) in which they detailed their expectations. Six characteristics appear in these treaties. The Book of Deuteronomy contains all six, including (1) a preamble; (2) a historical prologue; (3) stipulations of the treaty; (4) provisions for treaty renewal; (5) a calling upon divine witnesses; and (6) a series of blessings and curses.

1. Why do you think God would establish a covenant similar to a legal treaty with which His people were familiar?

2. Moses delivered his sermons at a major turning point in Israel's history. Describe that turning point.

Preamble

Read Deuteronomy 1:1–5. Suzerain/vassal treaties began with a preamble in which the suzerain identified himself to the vassal. Verse 1 contains the phrase "These are the words," Deuteronomy's ancient Hebrew title. In this case, God is the suzerain, and Moses spoke the preamble on God's behalf (v. 3).

3. Moses begins with details on Israel's location at the time of his sermons (vv. 1, 5). Where were they?

4. The Lord delayed Israel's entrance into the Promised Land for forty years (Numbers 14:26–45). He sometimes delays things in our lives. How might these delays prove beneficial?

Historical Prologue

Read Deuteronomy 1:6–18. A historical prologue is another characteristic of a suzerain/vassal treaty. Deuteronomy's historical prologue begins in verse 6 and concludes with 4:43.

5. God fulfilled His promise to Abraham (1:10; Genesis 15:5). How?

6. As Israel increased in numbers, Moses asked, "How can I bear by myself the weight and burden of you . . . ?" (v. 12). What solution did Moses implement (v. 13)? How might this solution provide relief in growing congregations today?

The Spies

Read Deuteronomy 1:19–25. Moses recounts sending twelve spies into the land of Canaan. All Israel waited at Kadesh-barnea, in the hill country of the Amorites, until the spies returned. Twelve spies were sent, one for each of the twelve tribes.

7. What would be the benefit of sending spies into Canaan? Why would God approve of such a practice?

8. The spies returned with a divided report. All reported that the land was "good" (v. 25). However, ten spies' hearts "melted" when they saw "great and fortified" cities (v. 28). What impact did their report have on the Israelites at Kadesh-barnea?

Rebellion against God

Read Deuteronomy 1:26–46. Rebellion against God brings consequences. Here we read a condensed version of Numbers 14. God disciplines those He loves in order that they may return in repentant faith to Him. Israel's rebellion costs them an entire generation of people.

9. Moses described the underlying cause of Israel's rebellion as a lack of belief (Deuteronomy 1:32). What does God provide you and me to strengthen our faith in Him?

10. God disciplined His people so that only two men of that generation, Caleb (v. 36) and Joshua (v. 38), entered the Promised Land. How did this nevertheless demonstrate God's grace?

Wandering

Read Deuteronomy 2:1–23. God disciplined Israel for rebelling. During her desert wandering, an entire generation died while a younger generation took their place. Yet, God graciously traced her every footstep (v. 7).

11. When did God say the time was right to begin Israel's conquest (vv. 16–18)?

12. God forbade Israel from fighting the people of Esau (v. 4), the Moabites (v. 9), and the Ammonites (v. 19). At this point in Israel's journey, how might even limited conflict have been dangerous (see v. 16)?

God's Word for Today

One of the central themes of Deuteronomy is God's faithfulness. While the Israelites often broke their promises to God, God never broke His.

13. Moses continually attributed Israel's victory over her enemies to God's hand of blessing. At the cross, Jesus defeated our chief enemies of sin, Satan, and death. Discuss how Jesus' death is the source of our strength when we fight the temptation to sin (1 Corinthians 10:13).

14. Paul writes, "all the promises of God find their Yes in [Jesus Christ]" (2 Corinthians 1:20). The Greek verb used here tells us that this was true in the past and is still true today. Discuss why Christianity means faith in God's promises.

In Closing

Encourage participants to begin the following activities:

- Using a Bible atlas or other reliable resource, retrace Israel's steps from Mount Sinai to Kadesh-barnea.
- List several ways that God has been faithful to you.
- Read Deuteronomy 2:24–3:29 to prepare for the next session.

Close by singing or reading together "From God Can Nothing Move Me" (*LSB* 713:1, 2, 7).

From God can nothing move me;
He will not step aside
But gently will reprove me
And be my constant guide.
He stretches out His hand
In evening and in morning,
My life with grace adorning
Wherever I may stand.

When those whom I regarded
As trustworthy and sure
Have long from me departed,
God's grace shall still endure.
He rescues me from sin
And breaks the chains that bind me.
I leave death's fear behind me;
His peace I have within.

For thus the Father willed it,
Who fashioned us from clay;
And His own Son fulfilled it
And brought eternal day.
The Spirit now has come,
To us true faith has given;
He leads us home to heaven.
O praise the Three in One!

Prayer: Heavenly Father, send Your Holy Spirit to guide our study of Your Word. May we know Your faithfulness, a faithfulness shown to the whole human race through the redemption won for us through Jesus Christ. You never waver in Your plan of salvation, for which we give you thanks and praise. Amen.

Lesson 2

You Belong to God

We can only imagine what the ancient Israelites experienced as they camped on the east side of the Jordan River. With their attention focused on Moses, they listened as he recounted to them God's faithfulness. God claimed them for Himself. He set them apart. He made them holy. Their response to God's gracious words and deeds was to keep His holy commands and decrees. As Moses' historical prologue continued, he reminded them of the events they knew well. They had participated in them. They had passed through the land of the Edomites and had skirted around the territory of the Moabites and the Ammonites.

The Israelites also knew well the ancestry of these people through whose territory they passed. With good cause God had said of them, "Do not contend" (Deuteronomy 2:5, 9, 19). God wanted no harm to come to the Edomites, Moabites, and Ammonites because they and the Israelites had a shared ancestry. Isaac's son Esau, who sold his birthright to his twin brother, Jacob, was patriarch of the Edomites. Their territory ran south from the southern end of the Dead Sea to the Gulf of Aqaba, then eastward into the mountains. Prior to the time of Christ, Edom, known then as Idumea, produced Herod the Great. On the other hand, Abraham's nephew Lot was patriarch of the Moabites and Ammonites. Both tribes lived east of the Jordan River—the Moabites between the Zered and Arnon rivers and the Ammonites between the Arnon and Jabbok rivers.

Setting the Stage

The Arnon River empties into the Dead Sea at about its midpoint on the east side. Perhaps taking its name from the Hebrew word meaning "noisy," it makes its way for some 45 miles with a northwesterly flow. The entire nation of Israel crossed this 100-foot-wide river, its steep limestone embankment creating a treacherous descent. By God's hand, Israel successfully crossed the river and slowly inched toward the northern edge of the Dead Sea, some 1,378 feet below sea level.

15. Traveling by foot through the region east of the Jordan River was treacherous. Why might God have taken the Israelites this way and not by an easier route?

16. God protected the Edomites, Moabites, and Ammonites. Why?

Defeat of Sihon

Read Deuteronomy 2:24–37. Before the nation of Israel crossed the Arnon River, Moses sent messengers to Sihon, king of Heshbon. These messengers sought permission to cross Sihon's territory.

17. God promised Israel that "terror and dread" would grip the nations that opposed her (Exodus 15:16). How might God use "terror and dread" to bring people to Himself?

18. Both Sihon and Pharaoh stubbornly refused to yield to God's will. What can happen when people continually resist God's will (v. 30)?

Defeat of Og

Read Deuteronomy 3:1–11. With the defeat of Sihon, the Israelites continued their northward march toward the city of Bashan. Along the way, Og, king of Bashan, marched his army to meet Israel near the city of Edrei.

19. God encouraged Moses, telling him, "Do not fear him [king Og]" (v. 2). Can you recall a time when God encouraged you? If you feel comfortable doing so, share this event.

20. Israel's conquest was immense, spreading 140 miles south to north. Sixty fortified cities fell, as did numerous villages that were unprotected by walls. How was God working to prepare Israel for a victory across the river in Canaan? (See Joshua 2:8–11.)

Land Divisions

Read Deuteronomy 3:12–20. Moses' historical prologue included a retelling of Numbers 32 and 34:13–15. Three tribes asked Moses for land on the east side of the Jordan. In this case, Moses answers, "Yes, but . . . ."

21. Which tribes asked for land? What stipulation did Moses attach to the land?

Moses Cannot Enter Canaan

Read Deuteronomy 3:21–29. Moses related the sad account of why God would not permit him to cross into Canaan. Although his punishment might seem excessive to us, it does teach us a valuable lesson: no one, including Moses, is exempt from following God's holy laws. But even though Moses could not enter Canaan, God did permit him to view the Promised Land from the top of Mount Pisgah (Nebo).

22. What did Moses do to rouse God's anger?

23. Christians often face the painful reality of their struggle with sin. Sometimes, as in the case of Moses, the Lord's discipline seems harsh. The writer of Hebrews penned, "For the Lord disciplines the one He loves, and chastises every son whom He receives" (12:6). How are these words reassuring during those times when we are being disciplined by the Lord?

24. Whom did God appoint as Moses' successor (v. 28)? Had you been an Israelite, how might you have felt about God's decision?

25. What was Moses' responsibility toward his successor (v. 28)?

God's Word for Today

God's relationship with Moses was an intimate one. Moses could share his every thought and pray intercessory prayers on behalf of God's people, all the while knowing that God would hear him. We also have an intimate relationship with God—thanks to Christ.

26. Take a moment to reread Deuteronomy 3:23–26. Describe Moses' relationship with God.

27. Thanks to Jesus Christ, we, too, have an intimate relationship with God. In the Lord's Prayer, Jesus teaches us to call God "Father." What does this one word alone teach us about our relationship with God?

In Closing

Encourage participants to begin the following activities:

- Locate Baal-peor (Beth-peor) in a Bible atlas or other reliable resource.
- Discuss what happened at Baal-peor (Numbers 25:1–8).
- Read Deuteronomy 4:1–43 to prepare for the next session.

Close by singing or reading together "Salvation unto Us Has Come" (*LSB* 555:1–3, 10).

Salvation unto us has come
  By God's free grace and favor;
Good works cannot avert our doom,
  They help and save us never.
Faith looks to Jesus Christ alone,
Who did for all the world atone;
  He is our one Redeemer.

What God did in His Law demand
  And none to Him could render
Caused wrath and woe on ev'ry hand
  For man, the vile offender.
Our flesh has not those pure desires
The spirit of the Law requires,
  And lost is our condition.

It was a false, misleading dream
  That God His Law had given
That sinners could themselves redeem
  And by their works gain heaven.
The Law is but a mirror bright
To bring the inbred sin to light
  That lurks within our nature.

All blessing, honor, thanks, and praise
  To Father, Son, and Spirit,
The God who saved us by His grace;
  All glory to His merit.
O triune God in heav'n above,

You have revealed Your saving love;
  Your blessèd name we hallow.

Prayer: Merciful Father, grant us the peace of knowing Your salvation. Help us to see in the ministry of Moses a foreshadowing of an even greater Moses: our Savior, Jesus Christ. In His name. Amen.

Lesson 3

Set Apart by God

In human history, Israel's exodus from Egypt stands as a most spectacular event. Although the new generation that gathered around Moses by the Jordan had not experienced the event themselves, their parents and grandparents had. Undoubtedly, the retelling of God's deliverance in the exodus, along with the annual Passover observance, kept the event fresh in their minds. Yet, there is more to it than that. To the Jews, what their ancestors experienced, they experienced. Therefore, as Moses retold past events, the sons and daughters of the actual participants of the exodus relived the events as if they had been there themselves.

What makes Israel's exodus so historically unique? At no other time in history save one did God bring about salvation of His people on such a grand scale. To the Israelites enslaved in Egypt, God sent Moses, a man who, by his own admission, did not speak well (Exodus 4:10). Through miraculous signs and wonders, the Lord God proved His authority over creation. God's miracles culminated in lamb's blood smeared on doorposts; by the blood of the lamb, God spared the firstborn and emancipated one nation from another, claiming Israel as His own. At God's command, the Red Sea parted, providing safe passage for the Israelites, and then closed again around the pursuing Egyptian army (Exodus 14:26–28).

Only one other rescue comes with a greater—and eternal—impact, and it was a rescue foreshadowed by the deliverance of the Israelite nation. On the cross of Calvary, our Lord Jesus Christ effected an eternal rescue of humankind through the outpouring of His precious blood. This was not the Passover lamb roasted in Egypt and eaten in haste, but "the Lamb of God, who takes away the sin of the world"

(John 1:29). Jesus is "our Passover Lamb, [which] has been sacrificed" (1 Corinthians 5:7) for us.

Setting the Stage

An upcoming verse in Deuteronomy needs a special note. This verse points out Israel's uniqueness and reminds Christians of their dramatic rescue from sin. "For ask now of the days that are past, which were before you, since the day that God created man on the earth, and ask from one end of heaven to the other, whether such a great thing as this has ever happened or was ever heard of" (Deuteronomy 4:32). Israel was set apart for God's purpose—justified by the blood of the Lamb. On the east side of the Jordan, Israel listened as Moses continued preaching.

28. Daily we take God for granted by minimizing Jesus' sacrifice for our salvation. What steps can we take to prevent this from happening?

29. Why is it important that Christians tell the story of God's love through Christ to their children and grandchildren?

Baal-peor Reviewed

Read Deuteronomy 4:1–14. Moses spoke of an incident that involved them directly. This new generation forgot all about what God had done and would continue to do for them. We may scoff at how quickly the Israelites sinned against God, but are we any different? Sin by any other name remains sin.

30. Misconceptions easily develop when we add to or take away from God's Word. What happened at Baal-peor to those who had not "held fast to the Lord" as opposed to those who had (vv. 3–4)?

31. If you feel comfortable doing so, describe a time when someone you know found himself or herself "letting go of God." What happened?

32. God taught the Israelite nation His statutes and decrees so that they might take possession of the land He had given them. What other reason does God give Israel to "keep and do" His commands (vv. 6–8)? How does this additional reason relate to Jesus' command in Matthew 28:19–20?

No Idol Worship Allowed

Read Deuteronomy 4:15–40. When we think of the false religions of Canaan, idol worship should come to mind. Carved of wood or stone, these idols represented the many gods and goddesses of the Canaanite pantheon. The Canaanites thought that with human sacrifices, they could manipulate these gods to provide abundant crops, propagate livestock and children, and give them victory over their enemies.

33. The gods and goddesses of the Canaanites took many outward forms. What were some of them (vv. 16–18)?

34. With a few exceptions, which we will note in question 36, God prohibited His people from making any images to use in divine worship. Why? (See Exodus 20:3–6.)

35. What would happen if Israel made a "carved image in the form of anything" (v. 25)? And yet, if Israel abandoned false gods and returned to the Lord, how would God show His mercy (v. 31)?

36. God commanded the creation of golden cherubim to overlook the mercy seat of the ark of the covenant (Exodus 37:6–9), the embroidery of cherubim on the colorful curtain separating the Most Holy Place from the Holy Place in the tabernacle (Exodus 26:31–33; 36:35), and the creation and erection of Moses' bronze serpent (Numbers 21:4–9). To whom did these images point?

Cities of Refuge

Read Deuteronomy 4:41–43. After giving three Israelite tribes land east of the Jordan River, Moses set aside three cities as "cities of refuge." In the territory provided the tribe of Reuben, Bezer became their city of refuge. Ramoth in Gilead became the city of refuge for Gad, while Golan in Bashan became the city of refuge for Manasseh.

37. How were the cities of refuge another example of God's abundant mercy?

God's Word for Today

Sometimes we make idols of our own. These idols may not take the form of animals or birds, but we worship them just the same. Like the ancient Israelites, we wander away from God and suffer His loving discipline.

38. What idols might take our attention away from God?

39. God foreknew our sinfulness and provided for our return to Him. Christ gave the power to forgive sins—His "keys" (John 20:22–23)—to His Church on earth. What strength do you derive from the promise of forgiveness of sins?

In Closing

Encourage participants to begin the following activities:

- Think about what the term *moral law* might mean.
- Discuss what comes to mind when you think about the Ten Commandments.
- Read Deuteronomy 4:44–6:25 to prepare for the next session.

Close by singing or reading together "O God, Our Help in Ages Past" (*LSB* 733:1–4).

O God, our help in ages past,
Our hope for years to come,
Our shelter from the stormy blast,
And our eternal home:

Under the shadow of Thy throne
Thy saints have dwelt secure;
Sufficient is Thine arm alone,
And our defense is sure.

Before the hills in order stood
Or earth received her frame,
From everlasting Thou art God,
To endless years the same.

A thousand ages in Thy sight
Are like an evening gone,
Short as the watch that ends the night
Before the rising sun.

Prayer: Lord of the ages, we worship You alone. We hear Your voice each time we read Your holy Word. Be with us as our sure defense against idolatry. Father, You know how easily we are led astray; save us. We pray in the name of Jesus, our Lord. Amen.

Lesson 4

God's Moral Law

Travelers to Mount Sinai, at the southern edge of the Sinai Peninsula, can still trek to the top of the 7,498-foot peak where Moses received the Ten Commandments. Tracing the route known as *Sikket Saydna Musa* (the Path of Moses) takes about three hours, mounting a stairway of some 4,000 steps. A less-strenuous but also less-scenic route winds its way up the opposite side of the mountain.

While Moses stood on Mount Sinai, God carved into stone the moral laws He wanted His people to obey. These laws, in the simplest of terms, taught the Israelites how to live their lives in response to God's grace. The first three laws directed their attention to a respectful relationship with their God: to avoid idolatry; to respect God's name; and to worship on the Sabbath. The remaining commandments taught the Israelites how to live in community with one another: to honor parents; to protect human life; to remain sexually pure; to be truthful; and to respect another's spouse and property. Although God had imprinted His Law on human hearts at creation, to no other nation besides Israel did He given His written Law. Moses preached these laws as a new generation prepared to enter the land God had promised their ancestors.

"The Lord Spoke to You"

Those listening to Moses experienced what their ancestors experienced in the exodus. The original Passover was their Passover. The crossing of the Red Sea was likewise their crossing. Likewise, when Christians hear or read about the deeds of Christ, we are incorporated into them. Because of our Baptism into Christ's death and resurrection, Christ's Baptism is our Baptism. In the Lord's Supper, we do more than merely remember (however piously) Jesus' death on the cross. We are incorporated into His death, and we enjoy the benefits of His saving death by virtue of His body and blood, given and shed for us.

40. Paul wrote that God saved the Israelites "in the cloud and in the sea" (1 Corinthians 10:2) and provided their sustenance through food and drink, namely manna and the water that flowed from the rock (vv. 3–4). What truth can we derive from this passage?

41. Paul notes a little later (vv. 5–11) that God's discipline of these believers in the desert should serve to warn us against immoral and unspiritual behavior. What consequences does Paul note for those who receive the Lord's Supper unworthily (11:29–32)?

An Introduction

Read Deuteronomy 4:44–49. Moses reminded those assembled to hear him about the events of forty years earlier. Except for Caleb and Joshua, those who heard his sermon were a new generation. Moses begins the stipulations-and-commands portion of this covenant.

42. We recognize these stipulations and commands as God's Law. However, the word translated as "law" in verse 44 is *torah*, which means "teaching" or "instruction." How does this help us understand that it refers to all of God's Word, Law *and* Gospel?

The Ten Commandments

Read Deuteronomy 5:1–33. Moses commanded the hearing of God's moral laws as presented in the Ten Commandments. The agreement made with God at Sinai binds God to future generations, yet each generation should hear it repeated.

43. Should all of God's Word be taught to new generations? Why or why not?

44. God longs to shower blessings on His people. How does He ask them to respond to His generosity (v. 33)?

Love the Lord

Read Deuteronomy 6:1–25. In this section of Scripture, you will repeatedly come across words chiding Israel to teach "your son." God gives men, namely husbands and fathers, the responsibility to serve as the religious heads of their households. When the husband or father is not present or is unwilling or unable to do so, another person should take on the responsibility.

45. Devout Jews recognize Deuteronomy 6:4–9 as the *Shema*, which they pray twice daily. Jesus confessed the *Shema* in Mark 12:29. Why can we consider the *Shema* not only a prayer but also a statement of faith?

46. Moses warns that we should not "put the Lord your God to the test" (Deuteronomy 6:16). Jesus quoted this passage in response to Satan's temptations (Matthew 4:7). Why should we never try God's patience?

47. Our love for God does not earn our salvation. What is the real reason we Christians desire to love God as He commands? (For help with your answer, consult 1 John 4:19.)

God's Word for Today

By nature, we are sinners. We cannot keep God's Ten Commandments any more than the ancient Israelites could. Yet, we repent of our sins, and God forgives us for the sake of Christ. When God looks at believers, He no longer sees their sinfulness. Instead, He sees the righteousness of His Son (1 Corinthians 1:30).

48. How does God give us Christ's righteousness in exchange for our unrighteousness (Romans 3:21–22a)?

49. Jesus speaks of two natural responses to God's love for us in Matthew 22:36–40. What are they?

In Closing

Encourage participants to begin the following activities:

- Think about the phrase *The Lord alone is God.*
- Consider why it is important to pass on God's moral laws to future generations.
- Read Deuteronomy 9:7–11:32 to prepare for the next session.

Close by singing or reading together "Sing Praise to God, the Highest Good" (*LSB* 819).

Sing praise to God, the highest good,
   The author of creation,
The God of love who understood
   Our need for His salvation.
With healing balm our souls He fills
And ev'ry faithless murmur stills:
   To God all praise and glory!

What God's almighty pow'r has made,
  In mercy He is keeping.
By morning glow or evening shade
  His eye is never sleeping.
Within the kingdom of His might
All things are just and good and right:
  To God all praise and glory!

We sought the Lord in our distress;
  O God, in mercy hear us.
Our Savior saw our helplessness
  And came with peace to cheer us.
For this we thank and praise the Lord,
Who is by one and all adored:
  To God all praise and glory!

He never shall forsake His flock,
  His chosen generation;
He is their refuge and their rock,
  Their peace and their salvation.
As with a mother's tender hand,
He leads His own, His chosen band:
  To God all praise and glory!

All who confess Christ's holy name,
  Give God the praise and glory.
Let all who know His pow'r proclaim
  Aloud the wondrous story.
Cast ev'ry idol from its throne,
For God is God, and He alone:
  To God all praise and glory!

Prayer: Almighty and merciful Father, Your Ten Commandments show us our sin—serving as a curb, a guide, and a mirror for our lives. Strengthen us as we instruct future generations about Your grace and mercy. We pray through Your Son, Jesus Christ. Amen.

Lesson 5

Only by God's Righteousness

In our last lesson, we learned how God exhorted fathers to teach His laws to their children. Have you had a chance to think about why this may be important? Could it be that God knows our human nature perfectly well? He does! He knows that we can easily take Him for granted and forget the lessons He has taught us.

For a moment, recall the Passover. The Israelites painted blood on the doorposts of their homes, and the angel of the Lord "passed over" them. God instructed His people to celebrate the Passover annually, saying, "And when your children say to you, 'What do you mean by this service?' you shall say, 'It is the service of the LORD's Passover, for He passed over the houses of the people of Israel in Egypt'" (Exodus 12:26–27a). Teaching our children about God's grace ensures the spiritual health of future generations.

"What does this mean?" This question demonstrates *catechesis* at its most basic level. This Greek word means "to sound back and forth." The teacher asks a question, and the student repeats his or her answer, echoing back and forth until the lesson reaches its conclusion. Many Christian denominations use catechesis as a way of instructing their children; it is the style of instruction used by Martin Luther in 1529 in his Small Catechism.

A Who's Who in the Promised Land

The names of seven nations occupying the land of Canaan appear early in today's lesson. Who are these people called the Hittites, Girgashites, Amorites, Canaanites, Perizzites, Hivites, and Jebusites—known collectively as the Canaanites? Canaanites trace their lineage to

Noah's son Ham (Genesis 10:6, 15–18). The Canaanites settled along the Mediterranean Sea and the Jordan River. The Amorites settled on the southern slopes of the Judea mountains. The Jebusites lived in the mountain regions, making Jerusalem their capital city. The Hivites lived in the area around Mount Hermon and the Lebanon mountains. The Girgashites lived just west of the Jordan River, while the Perizzites, the least known of the seven Canaanite peoples, settled in the forests.

50. The Canaanites practiced spiritualism, divination, witchcraft, and human sacrifice. Why would God find such things detestable?

Drive Out the Canaanites

Read Deuteronomy 7:1–26. The seven nations occupying the Promised Land were noted by Moses as being "more numerous and mightier than yourselves" (v. 1). And yet, God commanded Israel to "take possession of it [the land]." We can almost imagine the Israelites saying, "We cannot do that!"

51. According to Moses, who would drive out the Canaanites (vv. 1–2)?

52. When faced with challenges in our lives, do we forget who ultimately comes to our aid? How can we prevent that from occurring?

53. God put eight items on His "do/do not do" list for Israel to abide by during the conquest of Canaan. What were these (vv. 2–5)?

54. God did not want the Israelites to intermarry with the Canaanites. Why (vv. 3–4)?

55. God wanted Israel to forcibly remove the pagan nations occupying the Promised Land because they hated Him (v. 10). What blessings did God promise for obeying His command (vv. 12–15)?

56. How might the Israelites have felt that day upon hearing Moses' words in verses 22–24?

Remember God

Read Deuteronomy 8:1–20. God cared for Israel's every need during their forty years in the wilderness. No detail escaped His loving eyes. While the Israelites wandered through the desert, God preserved something even more significant than their sandals (v. 4).

57. We wrongly imagine that by our own "power and might" we have "earned" wealth (v. 17). Why does God warn against such sinful boasting?

58. How would God discipline Israel if she turned her back on Him (vv. 19–20)?

God’s Righteousness

Read Deuteronomy 9:1–6. How tempting it was for Israel to say that her own righteousness had won favor with God! Yet, we also fall into this trap of self-righteousness by thinking, Because I’ve done this or that, I have earned God’s favor.

59. How did God speak of Israel’s self-righteousness? What two reasons did God give for choosing the Israelites to drive out the other nations (v. 5)?

The Golden Calf and Kadesh-barnea Remembered

Read Deuteronomy 9:7–29. If the Israelites wanted to stand on the record of their own righteousness, Moses reminded them of their previous unrighteous behavior. The events surrounding the golden calf and Kadesh-barnea received special mention.

60. What actions did Moses take on both occasions that saved the Israelites’ lives (9:18, 25–28)?

God’s Word for Today

Like the Israelites, we often believe that our righteous behavior merits God’s favor. We selectively sweep our unrighteous thoughts, words, and deeds under the rug and pretend that they did not happen. Then, like the Israelites, we need an intercessor.

61. Who intercedes before God on our behalf (Romans 8:26–27)?

62. How do you feel knowing that God has provided an intercessor to pray on your behalf?

63. Why is it important to acknowledge that God saved us by His righteousness through His Son—not through our own righteousness (Ephesians 2:8)?

In Closing

Encourage participants to begin the following activities:

- Consider why God might continue to remind Israel of her unrighteous behavior.
- Think about the significance of being familiar with the past so that you do not make the same mistakes.
- Read Deuteronomy 10:1–11:32 to prepare for the next session.

Close by singing or reading together "O Bless the Lord, My Soul" (*LSB* 814).

O bless the Lord, my soul!
  Let all within me join
And aid my tongue to bless His name
  Whose favors are divine.

O bless the Lord, my soul,
  Nor let His mercies lie
Forgotten in unthankfulness
  And without praises die!

'Tis He forgives thy sins;
  'Tis He relieves thy pain;
'Tis He that heals thy sicknesses
  And makes thee young again.

He crowns thy life with love
  When ransomed from the grave;
He that redeemed my soul from hell
  Hath sov'reign pow'r to save.

He fills the poor with good;
He gives the suff'rers rest.
The Lord hath judgments for the proud
And justice for th' oppressed.

His wondrous works and ways
He made by Moses known,
But sent the world His truth and grace
By His belovèd Son.

Prayer: Dear Lord, keep us mindful of Your grace shown through Christ Jesus at Calvary. His righteousness alone has saved us. We have no right standing before You apart from the righteousness You provide us freely through Your Son. Thank You for Your precious gift. Amen.

Lesson 6

New Tablets

After Moses in anger destroyed the original stone tablets God carved on Mount Sinai, God carved a second set and had them placed in the ark of the covenant. In suzerain/vassal treaties, it was common practice to store a covenant in a secure place for future reference. The ark measured almost 4 feet long, 2¼ feet high, and 2¼ feet wide. It was built of acacia wood and was covered with pure gold. Attached to the ark were four gold rings through which two acacia-wood carrying poles—also covered in gold—were inserted. A lid of pure gold covered the top of the ark. On this lid, two solid-gold cherubs faced each other, their outstretched wings touching. Inside the ark, Moses placed Aaron's budded staff, the tablets containing the Ten Commandments, and a golden jar filled with manna (Hebrews 9:4). Levitical priests carried the ark on their shoulders using the gold-covered poles. Whenever the Israelites traveled, the ark led the way, going some distance ahead as the reminder of God's gracious presence among the Israelite tribes.

God met with Moses and spoke with him at the ark of the covenant, the ark serving as the location of God's special presence on earth (Exodus 25:22). The Lord concealed His presence (*shekinah*) in a cloud (Exodus 24:16), which guided the Israelites both day and night (Exodus 40:35). Because of the Lord's gracious presence, the ark of the covenant became the focal point of atonement sacrifices during the festival of Yom Kippur (Leviticus 16:2).

Atonement through Christ

Our study today centers on Moses and the second stone tablet God carved and had placed in the ark of the covenant. However, before we begin, a quick look forward is in order. The ancient Israelites celebrated their release from sin during Yom Kippur. This festival and its rites foreshadowed the world's atonement from sin at Calvary, when Christ shed His blood once for all. The author of Hebrews writes, "He [Jesus Christ] entered once for all into the holy places, not by means of the blood of goats and calves but by means of His own blood, thus securing an eternal redemption" (9:12).

64. Why is it important to study the Old Testament types and figures of Christ such as we see in Yom Kippur?

65. Archaeologists and treasure hunters continue to search for the lost ark of the covenant. How would finding the ark impact your faith?

New Tablets

Read Deuteronomy 10:1–11. In ancient times, each party to an agreement received a copy of the agreement they ratified—two tablets, one copy per party. This enabled both parties to "keep an eye" on the covenant. God placed both copies in the ark.

66. Since the ark was the place of God's special presence among His people, in reality, who was "keeping an eye" on the Ten Commandments contained in it?

67. Aaron the high priest died and was buried (v. 6). Who was his successor?

68. How did God provide for the priests that served in the tabernacle, given the fact that they received no land inheritance in Canaan (v. 9)?

Fear the Lord

Read Deuteronomy 10:12–22. In His mercy, God set the nation of Israel apart from other nations. Through Moses, God reminded them of what He had graciously done for them and, in turn, what He expected from them. God's instructions seem a good deal like a father's instructions to his dear children.

69. Match each of God's expectations on the left with its corresponding Bible passage on the right.

a. Fear the Lord.	___verse 12b
b. Walk in His ways.	___verse 12c
c. Love Him.	___verse 12d
d. Serve Him with heart and soul.	___verse 13
e. Keep His commands and statutes.	___verse 12a

70. God commanded the Israelites to "love the sojourner." What significance did God place behind this command (v. 19)?

71. Is swearing by any other name but the Lord's name idolatry (v. 20)?

Love and Obey God

Read Deuteronomy 11:1–32. Systematically, God reminded Israel that the privilege of bearing His name—"God's chosen people"—also came with the responsibility of following His laws. If His people kept these laws, God would continue to shower Israel with His blessings

(vv. 8–9, 13–15). Suzerain/vassal treaties contain similar blessings and curses. When a vassal agreed to a covenant, he accepted both the blessings and curses found in the agreement. We will examine the specific details of the blessings and curses in an upcoming lesson.

72. What made the land of Canaan different from that of Egypt (vv. 10–12)?

73. What curses would God bring down on Israel should they "turn aside and serve other gods" (vv. 16–17)?

74. Do God's curses seem harsh to you? Explain.

75. Israel had no organized army for the monumental task of driving the Canaanites out of the Promised Land. What did God promise in this regard (vv. 22–25)? Would you have found these words reassuring? Why or why not?

76. Later, God would establish an elaborate covenant ceremony in Canaan with details only hinted at in Moses' sermon (v. 29). Why do you think God wanted Israel to erect permanent monuments containing His blessing and curses?

God’s Word for Today

God set the Israelites apart from those nations occupying the land of His promise. He gave them His laws to teach them how to live in community with Him and their fellowman. Similarly, God sets Christians apart from non-Christians (1 John 2:15).

77. Jews believe that Judaism is more than a religion—it is a way of life. What difference might we see in the world if Christians viewed their religion in the same manner as Jews view theirs?

78. Through Holy Communion, God has provided you and me with a powerful reminder of Christ’s cruel death on our behalf. Each time we eat Christ’s body and drink His blood, we do so “in remembrance” of Him. What blessing does the Lord’s Supper bring? What curses accompany improper eating and drinking (1 Corinthians 11:29)?

In Closing

Encourage participants to begin the following activities:

- Locate Mount Gerizim and Mount Ebal in a Bible atlas or other reliable resource.
- Consider what it means to “fear the Lord.”
- Read Deuteronomy 12–14 to prepare for the next session.

Close by singing or reading together “Not What These Hands Have Done” (*LSB* 567:1–3, 6).

Not what these hands have done
  Can save this guilty soul;
Not what this toiling flesh has borne
  Can make my spirit whole.

Not what I feel or do
  Can give me peace with God;

Not all my prayers and sighs and tears
  Can bear my awful load.

Thy work alone, O Christ,
  Can ease this weight of sin;
Thy blood alone, O Lamb of God,
  Can give me peace within.

I bless the Christ of God,
  I rest on love divine,
And with unfalt'ring lip and heart
  I call this Savior mine.

Prayer: Father of all grace, You gave us Your own Son as the atoning sacrifice for our sins. Help us never to forget what You have done for us. Send Your Spirit to set us apart from a world filled with sin so that others may come to know You. We pray in Jesus' name. Amen.

Lesson 7

God's Ceremonial Law

When many people speak of God's Law, they have in mind only God's moral law as expressed in the Ten Commandments. However, in the Old Testament, God's laws included much more than a simple list of ten dos and don'ts. In addition to the moral law, God commanded the Israelites to obey the civil law. Further, God gave His people ceremonial law to make them "a kingdom of priests and a holy nation" (Exodus 19:6). How can any nation stand in purity before God if He has not provided them the means to do so? The ceremonies God instituted both purified His people and pointed forward in time to Christ, for such ceremonies were "a shadow of the things to come" (Colossians 2:17).

Moses had given God's people His ceremonial law once before. Now that that generation had passed, a new generation had gathered to hear Moses speak this law once again. The portion of Deuteronomy we will now study does not list all of the ceremonial laws, so we will look at them only briefly. The seven areas of ceremonial law had to do with the dedication of the firstborn and giving of firstfruits (Exodus 13:2, 12–13; 22:29–30); clean and unclean food (Leviticus 11); the rites of purification (Leviticus 12–15); disfigurement and tattooing (Leviticus 19:28); unlawful sexual relations (Leviticus 18); governing the Levites (Numbers 3:5–13); and establishing the dates for feasts and sacred days (throughout Exodus, Leviticus and Numbers).

Fulfillment in Christ

Keeping the whole Law—moral, civil, and ceremonial—was a strenuous task. While only the moral law was written on man's heart at creation, God expected His chosen people to obey also those state laws pertaining to the governance of the Israelites, and the laws that regulated religious practice in the Old Testament.

As Christians, we may offer a prayer of thanksgiving knowing that Jesus Christ fulfilled the Law on our behalf: "But when the fullness of time had come, God sent forth His Son, born of woman, born under the law, to redeem those who were under the law, so that we might receive adoption as sons" (Galatians 4:4–5). While we strive with the Spirit's help to obey the moral law, in Christ we are set free from the commands of the Old Testament civil and ceremonial laws, as they, too, have been fulfilled in Him.

79. To what reality did all of the Old Testament ceremonial law point (Colossians 2:16–17)?

80. Is there any value to Christian ceremonies that are observed in Christian freedom and that magnify Christ? Why or why not? If there is, what are some examples?

Holy Worship

Read Deuteronomy 12:1–32. The Canaanites practiced polytheism (the worship of many gods). Large, upright boulders placed near their altars represented their male god, Baal. Wooden poles represented their female goddess, Asherah.

81. Another practice among the Canaanites was the drinking of animal blood. What did God command about the blood of sacrifices and slaughtered animals (vv. 16, 23–27)?

82. The blood of animals sacrificed to God had a special purpose. How was it used (Leviticus 17:11)?

83. To whom did animal sacrifice and the sanctity of blood point? (See Hebrews 9:11–15.)

84. Holy worship had another unique feature. In Canaan, the residents of each city chose the gods they would follow; the Israelites, on the other hand, sought the one place where God would choose to put His name (v. 5). What were the Israelites to do to pagan centers of worship (vv. 2–3)?

"False Prophets"

Read Deuteronomy 13:1–18. Soon the temptation to worship other gods would increase. Across the Jordan River, the Israelites were about to encounter seven pagan nations with numerous gods and goddesses, just as in the Egyptian culture they had left behind. God warned the Israelites about the upcoming temptation.

85. How were the Israelites to respond when a "prophet or a dreamer of dreams" performed a sign and told them to follow other gods (vv. 1–4)?

86. What was the punishment for anyone trying to entice someone away from God's love and salvation (v. 5)?

87. How did God address the issue of an unfaithful city (vv. 12–18)?

88. Do you think false prophets exist today? Why or why not? What did Jesus say about false prophets (Matthew 24:24–26)?

89. What did Paul recommend for Christians confronted by false prophets (Romans 16:17)?

Clean and Unclean Food

Read Deuteronomy 14:1–21. Moses restated God's laws concerning "clean" and "unclean" food. First, Moses listed six clean animals that the Israelites were permitted to eat. Pigs were among the unclean animals. Historians tell us that the Canaanite cultures sacrificed pigs, as did the Egyptians and the Babylonians.

90. By what criteria were animals and birds judged "clean" or "unclean" (vv. 6–21)? What did these designations mean to an Israelite?

Tithing

Read Deuteronomy 14:22–29. Every Israelite was required to bring a tithe to the central area of worship. The tithe included grain, wine, oil, and the firstborn of the flocks. If an Israelite lived too far from the central worship location, he could exchange the tithe for money and then deliver the money to the place of worship.

91. Tithing is not a requirement for the New Testament Church. Instead, we are instructed that "each one must give as he has decided in his heart, not reluctantly or under compulsion" (2 Corinthians 9:7). Nevertheless, what might our level of giving indicate about our spiritual life?

92. To whom was the tithe of grain in the third year to be given (v. 29)? Are there members of your congregation or community who could benefit from a similar ministry?

God's Word for Today

You can easily see why God's laws caused many Israelites to long for the days of the coming Messiah. Looking at law upon law and seeing how sinful they were when compared to those laws must have been daunting.

93. Instead of offering animal sacrifices to the Lord, as the ancient Israelites did, what may Christians offer instead (Hebrews 13:15–16)?

94. What are some practical ways you could "present your bodies as a living sacrifice, holy and acceptable to God" (Romans 12:1)?

In Closing

Encourage participants to begin the following activities:

- Learn more about the sabbatical year in a Bible dictionary or other reliable source.
- Consider the significance of the Passover in the life of an Israelite.
- Read Deuteronomy 15:1–16:17 to prepare for the next session.

Close by singing or reading together "Rejoice, My Heart, Be Glad and Sing" (*LSB* 737:1, 2, 5, 6).

Rejoice, my heart, be glad and sing,
  A cheerful trust maintain;
For God, the source of ev'rything,
  Your portion shall remain.

He is your treasure, He your joy,
  Your life and light and Lord,
Your counselor when doubts annoy,
  Your shield and great reward.

He only will with patience chide,
   His rod falls gently down;
And all your sins He casts aside
   In ocean depths to drown.

His wisdom never plans in vain
   Nor falters nor mistakes.
All that His counsels may ordain
   A blessèd ending makes.

Prayer: Heavenly Father, Your Law shows us our sin. Yet, in Your grace, You have saved us, for Your Son kept Your Law perfectly for us. Help us always to serve You in thankfulness for His willing obedience. In Jesus' name. Amen.

Lesson 8

Celebrating God's Grace

God's abundant grace toward the Israelites was evident in His careful grooming of a new generation; in the leadership He provided through Moses; in the conquest of the lands east of the Jordan; and in His daily satisfying of their physical needs. Truly, God desired the Israelite nation to serve as an example and a witness to other nations. To remind the Israelites of His gracious words and deeds, God mandated several feasts and festivals so that His people might come before Him and worship Him in faith. In this lesson, we will look at four such festivals: the sabbatical year; the Passover; the Feast of Weeks; and the Feast of Booths.

Perhaps you are most familiar with the Passover. The contemporary Jewish Seder meal may be somewhat like the Passover meal Jesus celebrated with His disciples on the night in which He was betrayed. Matthew writes that "Jesus took bread, and after blessing it broke it and gave it to the disciples, and said, 'Take, eat; this is my body' " (Matthew 26:26). Jesus also took the cup, "and when He had given thanks He gave it to them, saying, 'Drink of it, all of you, for this is my blood of the covenant, which is poured out for many for the forgiveness of sins' " (Matthew 26:27–28).

Christ, the True Redemption

For those gathered together around Moses, the fulfillment of the Lord's redemptive work still remained years away. However, through the rites and ceremonies associated with Passover, God gave His people a foretaste of the redemption that awaited the world. The Passover served both as a memorial to what God had done in Egypt and as a preview of what God would do through His Son at Calvary. In between these two ages—the age of Passover and the age of its fulfillment in Christ—God's people would walk through times of forgetfulness and complacency. But God never forgot the solemn promise of a Savior He made to Adam and Eve (Genesis 3:15) and renewed with Abraham, Isaac, and Jacob. He fulfilled that promise in Christ Jesus, our Lord.

95. How might knowing the Old Testament background of the Passover help you better appreciate Holy Communion?

96. In what ways do meals and table fellowship help strengthen relationships in families? in congregations?

Cancelled Debts

Read Deuteronomy 15:1–11. Moses continued his speech to the Israelites with a restatement of God's command for a sabbatical year. Occurring every seven years, the sabbatical year contained special provisions including the canceling of debts.

97. What benefits would arise from a festival in which the debts of all people were cancelled?

Servants Freed

Read Deuteronomy 15:12–18. Israelites were prohibited from becoming the lifelong slaves of their fellow countrymen. If an Israelite sold himself into servanthood to a fellow Israelite, he knew that, by the Lord's direction, the situation would only be temporary.

98. How long could an Israelite hold a fellow Israelite in servitude (v. 12)?

99. An Israelite slave owner was obligated to care for his fellow Israelites after he freed them. What was the former slave owner to do (v. 14)?

100. God called upon the Israelites to "remember that you were a slave in the land of Egypt, and the LORD your God redeemed you" (v. 15). If the Israelites constantly held this thought in mind, how might it temper their treatment of their fellowman held in servitude?

Firstborn Animals

Read Deuteronomy 15:19–23. All firstborn male animals belonged to God. The Israelites presented firstborn animals without blemish as sacrifices before the Lord, and they ate their cooked flesh as part of a communal meal.

101. How did the Jews treat unblemished animals within the herd (vv. 19–20)? How was this different from the way they treated blemished animals (vv. 21–22)?

102. Verse 23 restates the prohibition against eating blood. Some pagan cultures drank blood because they believed that they received the animal's power through its blood. God used blood to redeem His people in Egypt; He would use it again to ransom His people from sin. What did Christ's words from the cross written in John 19:30 have to do with this ransom?

Passover

Read Deuteronomy 16:1–8. The Israelites celebrate Passover each year during the month of Abib, the first month of the Hebrew calendar, which corresponds roughly to our March or April. The Passover commemorates God's deliverance of the Israelite nation from out of Egypt.

103. In Deuteronomy 16:2–8 you will find nine regulations governing Passover. Look closely; what are they?

Feasts

Read Deuteronomy 16:9–17. Moses mentions two other feasts: the Feast of Weeks, also known as Pentecost, and the Feast of Booths, which received its name from the temporary structures the Israelites built to live in during the celebration. (Many Jews still do this today.) Pentecost occurred fifty days after Passover—in our May or June—while the Feast of Booths occurred in our month of September or October.

104. The Feast of Weeks celebrated the beginning of harvest, and the Feast of Booths marked the harvest's completion. Why were both occasions appropriate times to honor God?

God's Word for Today

God gave the Israelites feasts and festivals as memorials to His saving words and deeds. In freedom, Christians hold feasts and festivals such as Christmas and Easter to remember the blessings that Christ earned for us with His sacrificial life, death, and resurrection.

105. What two "memorials" of Christ's death and resurrection did He institute so that we would remember His sacrifice? (See Romans 6:3–6 and 1 Corinthians 11:23–26.)

106. God established the Passover in order to remind the Israelites within the context of a meal that a lamb's blood was shed for them in order to rescue them from death and domination. How does this help you better understand Holy Communion?

In Closing

Encourage participants to begin the following activities:

- List other ways God reminds us of His blessings.
- Learn more about the pagan gods of Canaan by consulting a Bible dictionary or other reliable resource.
- Read Deuteronomy 16:18–18:13 to prepare for the next session.

Sing or read together "I Love Your Kingdom, Lord" (*LSB* 651).

I love Your kingdom, Lord,
The place of Your abode,
The Church our blest Redeemer saved
With His own precious blood.

Beyond my highest joy
I prize its heav'nly ways,
Its sweet communion, solemn vows,
Its hymns of love and praise.

I love Your Church, O God,
Your saints in ev'ry land,
Dear as the apple of Your eye
And graven on Your hand.

For them my tears shall fall;
For them my prayers ascend;
For them my cares and toils be giv'n
Till toils and cares shall end.

Sure as Your truth shall last,
  To Zion shall be giv'n
The brightest glories earth can yield
  And brighter bliss of heav'n.

Prayer: Heavenly Father, You show us Your mercy. Never let us take Your love for granted. Send Your Holy Spirit to remind us of Your love and grace, which You share with us in Holy Baptism and Holy Communion. In Jesus' name. Amen.

Lesson 9

God's Civil Laws

Moses continued his sermon to the Israelites on the east side of the Jordan. In this lesson, we learn God's plan for civil laws, comprising the third portion of the stipulations God handed down through Moses. The Israelites could appoint judges and officials in their own towns (Deuteronomy 16:18), but what about cases of life and death? Such high-profile cases fell under Levitical jurisdiction (17:8).

Who were the Levites, the men to whom God entrusted so much? The Levitical order came from Levi, the son of Jacob (Genesis 29:34). All descendants of Levi's three sons—Gershon, Kohath, and Merari—became the Levites, with the exception of Kohath's grandson, Aaron. Aaron and his sons served the Lord as His priests.

The Levites' assigned tasks included every detail of the movement of the ark of the covenant (Numbers 3:5ff). They camped nearest the ark whenever Israel stopped marching. Each Levitical tribe was assigned a specific location to encamp—the Gershonites to the west of the ark (Numbers 3:23), the Merarites to the north (Numbers 3:35), the priests on the east side (Numbers 3:38), and the Kohathites to the south (Numbers 3:29). Levites attended the priests and assisted them during worship services (Numbers 8:19). They did not serve in the military and were not counted by any census (Numbers 1:47). In Canaan, the Levites took possession of forty-eight cities, in effect scattering themselves among God's people to care for their country-men's spiritual well-being.

A Solid Foundation

In His grace, God worked to protect His people from spiritual harm. When the Israelites entered the Promised Land, God did not allow them to fend for themselves, religiously speaking. Instead, God instituted a central place of worship. In addition, God instituted a judicial process to protect His people from themselves. Unlike the judicial system we recognize today, with a judge overseeing a case and a jury determining the verdict, the Israelite judicial system was overseen by elders or priests. Under this system, at least two eyewitnesses were required to prove guilt. When necessary, priests also comprised something similar to a court of appeals.

107. What would you think about a court system based solely on God's laws and not man's?

Judges and False Gods

Read Deuteronomy 16:18–17:7. Here we find the restatement of civil order as first suggested by Moses' father-in-law (Exodus 18:13–26).

108. Each town in the Promised Land could appoint its own "judges and officers" (Deuteronomy 16:18). What requirements did Moses set in place for these officials (vv. 19–20)?

109. Asherah poles were carved out of wood and bore the likeness of the pagan goddess Asherah. Sacred stones represented Astarte and Baal, female and male deities worshiped by the Canaanites. Why would God find these images offensive? (See Exodus 20:3.)

110. The penalty for worshiping false gods, or "transgressing [God's] covenant" (Deuteronomy 17:2), was death (v. 5). Why would God command His people to "purge the evil from your midst" (v. 7)?

111. Would you say that the worship of false gods remains a problem today? What are some of the false gods someone could worship?

Courts and Kings

Read Deuteronomy 17:8–20. God spelled out what to do with difficult legal questions and detailed His requirements for any king to rule over Israel. God knew what struggles Israel would experience after they stood before Samuel and demanded, "Appoint for us a king to judge us like all the nations" (1 Samuel 8:5).

112. To whom was Israel to turn in order to resolve legal questions "too difficult for [them]" (Deuteronomy 17:9)? What penalty applied to those not following the ruling of these men (v. 12)?

113. Match God's qualifications for a human king on the left with the corresponding Bible passage on the right.

a. God will choose the king.	___verse 18
b. He must not be a foreigner.	___verse 16b
c. He must not acquire many horses.	___verse 15a
d. The king shall not cause a return to Egypt.	___verse 17a
e. The king shall not have many wives.	___verse 16a
f. The king shall not acquire excessive silver and gold.	___verse 17b
g. The king shall write down God's laws.	___verse 15b
h. The king shall read God's laws daily.	___verse 19

114. Several Israelite kings should have come to mind when you read the restriction about "many wives," "acquiring many horses," and "acquiring excess gold and silver." Which are those? Why do you think God placed these restrictions on future kings?

Priestly and Levitical Offerings

Read Deuteronomy 18:1–8. Although the Levites and priests received no land inheritance when they entered Canaan, everyone else did. These men did not have to fend for themselves, however, for God provided for them. God's priests and the Levites received recompense for their services.

115. How did God provide for His priests and Levites (vv. 3–8)?

Deplorable Practices

Read Deuteronomy 18:9–14. Numerous pagan tribes inhabited the Promised Land. When we read of their religious practices and amoral behavior, we turn away in disgust. God abhorred their practices and sought to protect His chosen people from them. Specific "abominable practices of those nations" are mentioned in our text.

116. What are these "abominable practices" (vv. 10–14)?

117. How many of these "abominable practices" are still practiced today? by those claiming to be Christians?

God's Word for Today

Israel's kings—and hence, the guidelines—foreshadow Christ, although all of Israel's kings fell woefully short of God's will. Consider the first two kings, Saul and David. Saul turned his back on God, and David took numerous wives, committed adultery, and was guilty of premeditated murder. The major difference between the two is that David sought and received God's forgiveness in repentant faith.

118. What kingly characteristics does Christ model for us in Mark 10:45, John 5:30, and 1 Timothy 1:15?

119. We often call Jesus a "servant king." What is the difference between the usual human king and a servant king?

In Closing

Encourage participants to begin the following activities:

- Find information about "the Prophet" in a Bible dictionary or other reliable resource.
- Learn about cities of refuge by consulting a Bible dictionary or other reliable resource.
- Read Deuteronomy 18:14–22:12 to prepare for the next session.

Sing or read together "Beautiful Savior" (*LSB* 537:1, 3, 4).

Beautiful Savior,
King of creation,
Son of God and Son of Man!
Truly I'd love Thee,
Truly I'd serve Thee,
Light of my soul, my joy, my crown.

Fair is the sunshine,
Fair is the moonlight,
Bright the sparkling stars on high;
Jesus shines brighter,
Jesus shines purer
Than all the angels in the sky.

Beautiful Savior,
Lord of the nations,
Son of God and Son of Man!
Glory and honor,
Praise, adoration
Now and forevermore be Thine!

Prayer: Precious Lord, in Your mercy, You saw a world filled with sin, and You reached out Your hand to save it. In fact, You stretched out both of Your hands on Calvary's cross to restore us to Yourself. Thank You for Your great gift and holy sacrifice. In Your name. Amen.

Lesson 10

More Civil Laws

In Deuteronomy, we see a wonderful foreshadowing of the coming Messiah. In this session, we will hear Moses instruct the Israelites to keep watch for "a prophet like me from among you, from your brothers—it is to Him you shall listen" (Deuteronomy 18:15). As He did with Moses, God will speak directly to this Prophet (Numbers 12:8). To other prophets, God made himself known through dreams and visions (Numbers 12:6). In other words, this unique Prophet of God will speak with God face-to-face, as Moses did. Besides being a prophet, Moses also served as a ruler/judge and a priest. You may recall how Moses presided over the installation of his brother Aaron as high priest (Leviticus 8). Moses was, therefore, prophet, priest, and king, foreshadowing the person and ministry of Christ.

The Prophet of whom Moses speaks is none other than our Lord. Jesus received an anointing as prophet (Acts 10:38) and was recognized as a prophet (Matthew 21:46). Like Moses, Jesus served as priest. While the work of Old Testament priests was imperfect, Jesus' priestly work and sacrifice were perfect (Hebrews 9:11–22). The Scriptures also point to Jesus' rule over creation (Matthew 11:27; Ephesians 1:22; Hebrews 2:8). God gave Moses a glimpse into the future—a future when God fulfilled all Old Testament prophecies in the person of Christ.

A Man Hung on a Tree

A second foreshadowing of Christ occurs in this session. Moses speaks prophetically that "a hanged man is cursed by God" (Deuteronomy 21:23). This brutal method of execution receives no other mention in the Old Testament. In fact, among God's people, the standard means of execution was stoning, not hanging. Years later, in his letter to the Galatians, Paul revisited Moses' words and applied them to Jesus. Paul wrote: "For it is written, 'Cursed is everyone who is hanged on a tree'—so that in Christ Jesus the blessing of Abraham might come to the Gentiles, so that we might receive the promised Spirit through faith" (Galatians 3:13–14). God laid the curse of the world's sins on Christ at Calvary.

120. According to this passage in Galatians, Jesus' cross was both a curse (for Him) and a blessing (for us). In what ways can you view the crosses that you bear as both curses and blessings?

The Prophet

Read Deuteronomy 18:15–22. In the heart of Deuteronomy, God placed a noteworthy messianic prophecy. Moses provided a way for recognizing God's promised Messiah, Jesus Christ.

121. This Prophet will speak God's own Word and speak in God's own name (vv. 18–19). What do these two characteristics reveal about the authority of this Prophet's Word?

122. Do you believe that false prophets exist today? How can you tell whether or not a prophet is from God (v. 22)?

Cities of Refuge

Read Deuteronomy 19:1–21. Three Transjordan cities were set up as cities of refuge. In addition, God would establish three more cities of refuge on the other side of the Jordan River.

123. Why did God space His cities of refuge evenly throughout the Promised Land (v. 6)? How did God show His mercy through the placement of the cities of refuge?

124. We read descriptions of two types of murder in our text: accidental (vv. 4–5) and premeditated (vv. 11–12). What outcome did God prescribe for each (vv. 6, 13)?

125. Paul wrote that "[government] is the servant of God, an avenger who carries out God's wrath on the wrongdoer" (Romans 13:4). If God establishes governments to enforce His will, who ultimately wields the sword of justice?

126. What responsibility did the elders of a city of refuge have if they discovered that one of their residents had committed premeditated murder (v. 12)?

Preparations for War

Read Deuteronomy 20:1–20. After they crossed into Canaan, and with the prospect of violent battles looming before them, the Israelites probably experienced some doubt: "Can we possibly win against such superior forces as the Canaanites?"

127. God offered reassuring words to the Israelites: "You shall not be afraid," "Let not your heart faint," "Do not fear or panic and be in dread of them [the Canaanites]." How would this comfort the Israelites?

128. God has given Christians a task of equal importance to that of the conquest of Canaan: "Go therefore and make disciples of all nations, baptizing them in the name of the Father and of the Son and of the Holy Spirit" (Matthew 28:19). In the battle for human salvation, are we fighting alone? (For help, see v. 20.)

Unsolved Murder and Other Provisions

Read Deuteronomy 21:1–22:12. God's sanctity for human life becomes self-evident in a series of ordinances regulating unsolved murders. Here He also sets regulations concerning, among other things, the marriage of captive women; the status of a firstborn son and a rebellious son; and the wearing of clothing usually worn by the opposite sex.

129. The Hebrew word for "atonement" (21:8) is *kaphar* (kuh-FAR), meaning "to cover." With the elaborate rite detailed in verses 1–7, God "covers" Israel's guilt so that she is no longer exposed to His justice. How might this help to deepen our understanding of what Christ did for us at Calvary?

God's Word for Today

As we mentioned, Moses' second sermon to the Israelites covered Deuteronomy 4:44–28:68. Perhaps you have noticed that in these verses, God restated ordinances that He had given earlier to remind the people of His will for their lives.

130. Take a moment to read Romans 3:22–25. What can you do to share the joy that God "passed over [your] former sins" with those you know?

In Closing

Encourage participants to begin the following activities:

- Consider how an Israelite might have felt when he or she looked at God's laws. Might it be different from how you feel? If so, how?
- Think about how much God loves you and that He sent His own Son to "cover" your sins.
- Read Deuteronomy 22:13–26:19 to prepare for the next session.

Sing or read together "Not What These Hands Have Done" (*LSB* 567:1–3).

Not what these hands have done
  Can save this guilty soul;
Not what this toiling flesh has borne
  Can make my spirit whole.

Not what I feel or do
  Can give me peace with God;
Not all my prayers and sighs and tears
  Can bear my awful load.

Thy work alone, O Christ,
  Can ease this weight of sin;
Thy blood alone, O Lamb of God,
  Can give me peace within.

Prayer: Dear Father in heaven, Moses provided us a glimpse of the world's Savior. Jesus is our Prophet, Priest, and King. Thank You for sending us Your precious Son and our Redeemer. In His name. Amen.

Lesson 11

Follow the Lord

Take a moment to think back to your own childhood. Do you recall specific rules that your parents or guardians set for you? Did they mention that the purpose of these rules was to keep you safe? Now think about God's Ten Commandments. God instituted these moral rules and other laws for His people to safeguard their moral, spiritual, and civil welfare. Can you say that God has the safety of His people in mind?

As a child, why did you strive to keep your parents' or guardians' rules? Was it simply because you knew that by doing so, you could "earn" their love? Perhaps so, but children do obey their parents' or guardians' rules as a *response* to their love. This is God's desire. His rules protect His people from the consequences of their own sinful desires. When the Israelites kept God's laws, they reflected God's love back to Him.

How easy it is for Christians to say, "Christ kept God's Law fully, so I don't have to." In and of itself, this statement is true—as it pertains to our salvation. The ceremonial laws, which required animal sacrifices, ended with Christ's sacrifice (Hebrews 9:26). So, too, the civil laws find fulfillment in Christ's obedience to them; likewise, God's moral rules. However, today, the Holy Spirit still leads us to obey God's moral rules as we understand them in the Ten Commandments, and when we do, we display a willingness to submit to God's authority in response to His love.

God, the Protector of Life

At the end of our last session, we read about God's rules concerning the care of His animal and human creatures. Those rules include regulations about taking the life of a mother bird along with her offspring and adding a parapet to the roof of a home (Deuteronomy 22:6–8). In these verses, God's love of life shines through. Taking a mother bird's life while she still (presumably) had other living offspring needing her care would be cruel. And while hot evening temperatures made sleeping on the roof common in the Middle East, parapets prevented people from rolling off in their sleep to almost certain death.

131. Paul wrote, "[Love] does not insist on its own way" (1 Corinthians 13:5). How does this passage illustrate God's care even down to what we consider the "insignificant details" of life?

132. Do you think it possible to learn gentleness and kindness through the treatment of animals? How so?

Sexual Immorality

Read Deuteronomy 22:13–30. God instituted marriage for male and female companionship and the procreation of children, and with it, He gave sexual intimacy. Since the fall into sin, marriage has become even more of a necessity to curb sinful human desire (1 Corinthians 7:2).

133. What happened to a man who accused his wife of infidelity before their marriage if his charges proved false (Deuteronomy 22:18–19)? to the woman if proven true (vv. 20–21)?

134. Among the pagan nations, sexual immorality ran rampant. What do the following verses from Deuteronomy 22 teach Israel (and you and me) about sexual immorality?

verse 22

verses 23–24

verses 25–27

verses 28–29

verse 30

135. How does the command "you shall purge the evil from your midst" (v. 21) sum up God's stance on sin? Do you think God has changed His mind on this subject? Why or why not?

Laws for Assembly and Camp

Read Deuteronomy 23:1–14. God graciously provided ordinances to protect the Israelites from making their assembly and campsite unholy. In this passage, we see that a holy God will not tolerate unholiness.

136. Whom did God exclude from assembling before Him (vv. 1–3)? Why weren't the Edomites and Egyptians excluded (v. 7)?

Other Laws

Read Deuteronomy 23:15–25:19. Among these ordinances we find a law forbidding an Israelite woman from becoming a cult prostitute and ordinances governing divorce and Levirate marriages.

137. What might God hope to achieve by making divorce difficult (24:4)?

138. Levirate marriages seem unusual. However, the ancient Hittites, Assyrians, and Greeks permitted them, as did cultures in parts of South America, Africa and India. What was a Levirate marriage, and why might God have permitted it for a time (25:5–10)?

139. In a time when merchants sometimes carried two stone measuring weights—a lighter weight for purchasing and a heavier weight for selling—God wanted the Israelites to treat each other fairly. What ordinance did God pass on to His people to protect them from sinning against Him (vv. 13–16)?

Firstfruits and Tithes

Read Deuteronomy 26:1–15. In thankfulness to God for delivering them from Egypt and keeping His promise to give them a new homeland, the Israelites brought their firstfruits and tithes to Him.

140. Why might God continually ask the Israelites to remember the things He had done for them?

141. Can you think of a time when Christ called upon His disciples to remember what He would do for them? (See Luke 22:14–21.)

142. What is it that we remember about what Christ has done? (See Matthew 26:28.)

Admonishments

Read Deuteronomy 26:16–19. The requirements—or stipulations—section of the second giving of God's Law (begun in Deuteronomy 4:4) ends here. Next, we note three verses warning the Israelites if they failed to keep their part of the agreement with God.

143. What did Israel agree to do (v. 17)? What did God agree to do (vv. 18–19)?

144. God calls those who keep His commandments "His treasured possession" (v. 18). In Titus, Paul wrote that Christ redeemed and purified us to make for "himself a people for His own possession" (Titus 2:14). How might our attitudes toward one another and God change if every believer realized that he or she is God's own possession?

God's Word for Today

Through the pouring out of Christ's blood, God made a new covenant with you and me (Luke 22:19–20). This new covenant provided far more than the Old Testament system of sacrifices could offer.

145. How was this new covenant sealed, sanctifying us and cleansing us from our sins (Hebrews 10:10)?

146. Why should we remember that we are God's possessions because God has accomplished our forgiveness through Christ?

In Closing

Encourage participants to begin the following activities:

- Think about how Holy Baptism and Holy Communion epitomize God's grace.
- In a Bible dictionary or other reliable resource, locate the city of Shechem and also Mount Ebal and Mount Gerizim.
- Read Deuteronomy 27:1–30:20 to prepare for the next session.

Sing or read together "The Law of God Is Good and Wise" (*LSB* 579:1–3).

The Law of God is good and wise
And sets His will before our eyes,
Shows us the way of righteousness,
And dooms to death when we transgress.

Its light of holiness imparts
The knowledge of our sinful hearts
That we may see our lost estate
And turn from sin before too late.

To those who help in Christ have found
And would in works of love abound
It shows what deeds are His delight
And should be done as good and right.

Prayer: Lord God, You desire that we live our lives in praise of You. We are Your people because of Christ's reconciling death on the cross. Through His death, You purified us and made us Your own. Forgive us our sins and strengthen our faith, that we may do Your will. Through Jesus Christ, our Lord. Amen.

Lesson 12

God’s Covenant Ratified

As a high-school youth instructor attempted to determine what his class knew and did not know at the beginning of the year, he asked a simple question: “What is the Gospel?” To his surprise, no one knew the answer. No one could relate to him the simple words of John 3:16: “For God so loved the world, that He gave His only Son, that whoever believes in Him should not perish but have eternal life.”

Sadly, this is a true story. Also sad is the attempt to sweep such words as *sin* and *repentance* from the Christian vocabulary. Without sin, we find no need for a Savior, and without a Savior, the Christian Church loses its reason for being. In some Christian worship services across the United States, the congregation never confesses its sins. I once asked why Confession and Absolution were missing from a worship service I attended. I was told, “We found that with all the other elements of our service, there wasn’t time to include Confession and Absolution and still complete worship in under one hour.”

How quickly we forget that we are sinners! Now we can begin to understand why Moses assembled God’s chosen people on the east side of the Jordan. Painstakingly, Moses reviewed with them God’s rules for living as a covenant community. He knew that without such reminders, they would quickly forget all God had taught them. But even more than that, Moses also reviewed with them God’s covenant, His promises of His grace and blessing.

Twin Peaks

Twenty-five miles north of Jerusalem stand Mount Gerizim and Mount Ebal. Mount Ebal, the taller of the two, stands on the north side of the Shechem Valley. Its slopes are barren and covered with gray rocks—perhaps symbolizing the curses God promised Israel if they abandoned His covenant. On the other side of the valley stands Mount Gerizim. Its tree-covered slopes may represent the rich promise of God's blessings if Israel kept her covenant with Him.

147. Mount Gerizim and Mount Ebal will play a role in a dramatic covenant-signing ceremony (Joshua 8:30–35). What two teachings of the Bible stand like these mountains in our lives as Christians? (See Romans 3:20 and 1:16.)

148. Have you encountered a worship service in which there was no confession of sin? If so, describe your experience and how it made you feel.

149. How might you respond to a person, Christian or not, who said that confessing one's sins is not necessary? (See 1 John 1:8–9.)

Mount Ebal

Read Deuteronomy 27:1–26. Moses chronicled the planned ratification of God's covenant in Canaan, including a ceremony during which the blessings and curses would be read aloud, as was done in suzerain/vassal treaties of Moses' day. Large stones covered with plaster would contain the "words of this law" (v. 3).

150. Which tribes stood on Mount Gerizim to "bless the people" (v. 12)? Which tribes stood on Mount Ebal to utter the curses contained in God's covenant (v. 13)?

151. Match the curse on the left with its corresponding Bible verse on the right.

a. curse against a man who makes an image to worship	___verse 17
b. curse against anyone who dishonors his father or mother	___verse 19
c. curse against anyone who moves his neighbor's land marker	___verse 22
d. curse against anyone who misleads the blind	___verse 25
e. curse against anyone who perverts justice	___verse 16
f. curse against anyone who lies with his father's wife	___verse 20
g. curse against anyone who lies with an animal	___verse 23
h. curse against anyone who lies with his sister	___verse 26
i. curse against anyone who lies with his mother-in-law	___verse 18
j. curse against anyone who strikes down his neighbor in secret	___verse 24
k. curse against anyone who takes a bribe to shed innocent blood	___verse 21
l. curse against anyone who does not confirm the words of this law	___verse 15

Mount Gerizim

Read Deuteronomy 28:1–14. Israelite tribes standing on the south side of the Shechem Valley will read aloud the blessings God promises to those who faithfully follow His commands. In keeping God's commandments, we do not earn God's blessings; rather, we keep them in loving response to God's love for us.

152. What blessings does God promise in the following verses in chapter 28?

verse 1

verse 3

verse 4

verse 5

verse 6

verse 7

verse 8

verse 9

verse 10

verse 11

verse 12

verse 13

More Curses

Read Deuteronomy 28:15–68. God could withdraw His blessings if Israel disobeyed His covenant. Among those withdrawn blessings would be God's protection; He would cause Israel "to be defeated before [their] enemies" (v. 25). Disobedience would cause other problems for Israel as well, but it would not cause God to withdraw His promise of a Messiah.

153. What would happen to Israel's land inheritance if they disobeyed God (vv. 49–50, 64)?

Renewal

Read Deuteronomy 29:1–29. Moses began his third address by again reviewing Israel's history. He warned them against following false gods and failing to keep God's commands.

154. Should Israel rebel and fall away from God, how would God use her rebellion to witness to other nations (vv. 25–29)?

Life or Death

Read Deuteronomy 30:1–20. God knows our penchant to sin, and yet, He still holds out His loving hand to welcome back those who return to Him in repentance. We call that grace.

155. Describe the grace God demonstrates in verses 1–4.

156. Returning to God brings restoration. What promises does God make (vv. 6–10)?

157. How can we say that belief in God comes down to the simple phrase *life or death*?

God's Word for Today

The phrase *life or death* applies to Christians as well. Jesus Christ made that clear when He said, "I am the way, and the truth, and the life. No one comes to the Father except through me" (John 14:6).

158. What does Peter's confession teach us about eternal life (John 6:68)?

In Closing

Encourage participants to begin the following activities:

- Spend some time thinking about the word *grace*.
- Learn more about the death of Moses from a Bible dictionary or other reliable source.
- Read Deuteronomy 31:1–34:12 to prepare for the next session.

Sing or read together "I Know That My Redeemer Lives" (*LSB* 461:1, 2, 8).

I know that my Redeemer lives;
What comfort this sweet sentence gives!
He lives, He lives, who once was dead;
He lives, my ever-living head.

He lives triumphant from the grave;
He lives eternally to save;
He lives all-glorious in the sky;
He lives exalted there on high.

He lives, all glory to His name!
He lives, my Jesus, still the same;
Oh, the sweet joy this sentence gives:
I know that my Redeemer lives!

Prayer: Merciful Father, by His death on the cross, Your Son won for us eternal life. By Your Holy Spirit, strengthen us to carry this truth to family, friends, and neighbors so that they might come to faith and enjoy life forever with You. In Jesus' name. Amen.

Lesson 13

Succession of Leadership

The stage is set for Moses' last days. Although of sound mind, Moses' body surely felt the effects of one hundred and twenty years of life (Deuteronomy 31:2). Moses' life divides easily into three forty-year periods: forty years living in Egypt; forty years tending sheep in Midian; and forty years leading God's chosen people.

How might Moses have felt as he looked out upon his people for the last time? Did his mind race back through all the joys and heartaches of leadership? What exactly did he see when he looked to the opposite shore of the Jordan River—the land flowing with milk and honey? We may never know the answers to these questions. What we *do* know is that Moses set a standard of devotion to God that few have met. In Moses, we see a picture of Christ.

When God told Moses that he would die without setting foot in the land across the Jordan, no protest crossed Moses' lips. Instead, he showed us the steadfast resolve of a man set on doing God's will—whatever that will might be. Christ demonstrated the same resolve. When facing certain death, Jesus Christ prayed, "not as I will, but as You will" (Matthew 26:39). Moses gives us a brief preview of our Savior, the One who was greater than Moses. (See Hebrews 3:1–6.)

God's Will—Is It Our Desire?

When faced with uncertain situations, it is difficult to place ourselves under God's will. As sinners, we will always find it difficult to surrender to all that God wants for our lives. In the Lord's Prayer, Jesus teaches us to ask of our Father, "Your will be done, on earth as it is in heaven" (Matthew 6:10). Each time we pray these words, we ask not so much to understand every aspect of God's will for our lives, but that He would grant us the gifts of faith, hope, and joy as we submit to it. At the end of his life, Moses accepted God's will, and so did our Lord. In faith, we ask the Holy Spirit to teach us to do likewise.

159. Why do you suppose it is so difficult to submit to God's will in our lives, even though we know that God means all things for our good?

Joshua

Read Deuteronomy 31:1–13. Moses has come to the end of his ministry. While uncertainty may have existed in the minds of some of the Israelites, God already had Israel's new servant in mind: Joshua.

160. Through Moses, God offered Joshua advice and reassurance (vv. 7–8). Had you been Joshua, how would God's words have strengthened you as you prepared to succeed Moses?

161. Suzerain/vassal treaties always included writing out two copies of the treaty, with each party receiving a copy. To whom did Moses entrust Israel's copy (v. 9)?

162. To prevent the Israelites from forgetting their covenant with God, how often were they commanded to read God's laws aloud?

Rebellion Foretold

Read Deuteronomy 31:14–29. Before the Israelites crossed the Jordan River into Canaan, God already knew that they would rebel and become unfaithful to Him.

163. What does it say about God that He knows our choices in advance, even our choices to sin, and yet continues to love us anyway?

Song of Moses

Read Deuteronomy 31:30–32:47. Moses taught this wonderful song to God's people, the Israelites. As you read this song, take note of the number of times God is called "the Rock" (32:4, 15, 18, 30–31).

164. How might "the Rock" symbolize God's faithfulness to Moses, to the Israelites, and to you and me?

165. In suzerain/vassal treaty disputes, the suzerain commonly listed the kindnesses he had shown his vassal. Can you find such a section in this song? If so, where?

166. When Israel rebels (and they do, repeatedly), God does not "wipe them from human memory" (v. 26). Why not? (See v. 27.)

Last Days of Moses

Read Deuteronomy 32:48–34:12. Before he died, Moses blessed each of the twelve tribes of Israel, much as Jacob did before he died (Genesis 49:1–28). Judah's blessing (Deuteronomy 33:7) asked for God's help fighting Judah's adversaries; it pointed ahead to the period of judges following Joshua's death, and to the time of Christ—Judah's greatest heir (Matthew 1:3, 16).

167. Where did Moses die, and who buried him (Deuteronomy 34:1–6)?

God's Word for Today

Deuteronomy ends with a powerful description of Moses, a man God used to do "signs and wonders" in Egypt and "great deeds of terror" before all Israel (vv. 10–12).

168. Moses' life pointed forward to the time of an even greater Prophet who performed miracles, signs, and wonders (Matthew 4:23–25; John 21:25). As great a servant of God as Moses was, in what ways was he exceeded by the Servant of servants, our Savior, Jesus Christ?

169. We may be tempted to glorify Moses, but he is not the real hero of Deuteronomy. Who is the real hero in Deuteronomy?

170. In the burning bush, God identified Himself as "I AM WHO I AM" or simply "I AM" (Exodus 3:14). Similarly, Jesus Christ spoke the words "I Am" to identify Himself as the God of Israel in phrases like "Before Abraham was, I Am" (John 8:58). How do you feel knowing that you worship the same God worshiped by Moses centuries ago, the God who completed His plan of salvation through the death and resurrection of Jesus Christ?

In Closing

Sing or read together "On What Has Now Been Sown" (*LSB* 921).

On what has now been sown
  Thy blessing, Lord, bestow;
The pow'r is Thine alone
  To make it sprout and grow.
Do Thou in grace the harvest raise,
And Thou alone shalt have the praise!

To Thee our wants are known,
  From Thee are all our pow'rs;
Accept what is Thine own
  And pardon what is ours.
Our praises, Lord, and prayers receive,
And to Thy Word a blessing give.

O grant that each of us,
  Now met before Thee here,
May meet together thus
  When Thou and Thine appear
And follow Thee to heav'n, our home.
E'en so, amen, Lord Jesus, come!

Prayer: Merciful Lord, may we see in Your Law a curb, a guide, and a mirror for our lives. May we always recall our sinfulness with disdain and then look with joy to Your Son, who, on Calvary's cross, delivered us into eternity with You. We pray in Jesus Christ. Amen.

Leader Notes

These notes are provided as a "safety net," a place to turn for help in answering questions and for enriching discussion. They will not answer every question raised in your class. Please read them, along with the questions, before class. Consult them in class only after exploring the Bible references and discussing what they teach. Please note the different abilities of your class members. Some will easily find the Bible passages listed in this study; others will struggle. To make participation easier, team up members of the class. For example, if a question asks you to look up several passages, assign one passage to one group, the second to another, and so on. Divide the work! Let participants present the answers they discover.

Preparing to Teach Deuteronomy

To prepare to lead this study, read through the Book of Deuteronomy. You might secure a good commentary on the book and read it over or read the introduction to the book in *The Concordia Self-Study Bible* or a Bible handbook. Several maps of the Old Testament world at about 1500–1400 BC would also help.

The materials in these notes are designed to help you in leading others through this portion of the Holy Scriptures. Nevertheless, this booklet is to be an aid to—and not a substitute for—your own study of and preparation for teaching the Book of Deuteronomy.

If you have the opportunity, you will find it helpful to make use of other biblical reference works in the course of your study. These two commentaries can be very helpful: J. A. Thompson, *Deuteronomy: An Introduction and Commentary* (Downers Grove, IL: IVP, 1972), and Mark E. Braun, *Deuteronomy, People's Bible Commentary* (Milwaukee: Northwestern Publishing House, 1993; reprinted by Concordia Publishing House, 2005). Although it is not strictly a commentary, the section on Deuteronomy in *The Word Becoming Flesh* by Horace Hummel (St. Louis: Concordia Publishing House, 1979) also contains much that is of value for the proper interpretation of this biblical book.

Group Bible Study

Group Bible study means mutual learning from one another under the guidance of a leader. The Bible is an inexhaustible resource. No one person can discover all it has to offer. In any class, many eyes see many things and can apply them to many life situations. As the leader, you should resist the temptation to "give the answers" and so act as an "authority." This teaching approach stifles participation by individual members and can actually hamper learning. As a general rule, the teacher is not to "give interpretation" but to "develop interpreters." Of course, there are times when you should and must share insights and information gained by your study and by your class members through the lesson. And you'll want to engage class members in meaningful sharing and discussion at all points, leading them to a summary of the lesson at the close. As a general rule, don't explain what the learners can discover by themselves.

Have a chalkboard and chalk or newsprint and marker available to emphasize significant points of the lesson. Rephrase your inquiries or the inquiries of participants as questions, problems, or issues. This provokes thought. Keep discussion to the point. List on the chalkboard or newsprint the answers given. Then determine the most vital points made in the discussion. Ask additional questions to fill gaps.

The aim of every Bible study is to help people grow spiritually, not merely in biblical and theological knowledge, but in Christian thinking and living. This means growth in Christian attitudes, insights, and skills for Christian living. The focus of this course must be the church and the world of our day. The guiding question will be this: What does the Lord teach us for life today through the Book of Deuteronomy?

Teaching the Old Testament

Teaching the Old Testament can degenerate into mere moralizing in which "do-goodism" becomes a substitute for the Gospel and sanctification gets confused with justification. Actually, the justified sinner is not moved by God's Law but by God's grace to a totally new life. His or her faith in Christ is always at work in every context of life. Meaningful personal Christianity consists of faith flowing from God's grace in Christ and is evidenced in love for other people. Having experienced God's free grace and forgiveness, the Christian daily works in his or her world to reflect the will of God for humanity in every area of human endeavor.

The Christian leader is Gospel oriented, not Law oriented. He or she distinguishes Law from Gospel. Both are needed. There is no clear Gospel unless we first have been crushed by the Law and see our sinfulness. There is no genuine Christianity where faith is not followed by life pleasing to God. In fact, genuine faith is inseparable from life. The Gospel alone creates in us the new heart that causes us to love God and our neighbor.

When Christians teach the Old Testament, they do not teach it as a "law book," but instead as books containing both Law and Gospel. They see the God of the Old Testament as a God of grace who, out of love, establishes a covenant of grace with His people (Deuteronomy 7:6–9) and forgives their sins. Christians interpret the Old Testament using the New Testament message of fulfilled prophecy through Jesus Christ. They teach as leaders who personally know the Lord Jesus as Savior, the victorious Christ who gives all believers a new life (2 Corinthians 5:17) and a new mission (John 20:21).

Pace Your Teaching

The lessons in this course of study are designed for a study session of at least an hour in length. If it is the desire and intent of the class to complete an entire lesson each session, it will be necessary for you to summarize the content of certain answers or biblical references in order to save time. Asking various class members to look up different Bible passages and to read them aloud to the rest of the class will save time over having every class member look up each reference.

Also, you may not want to cover every question in each lesson. This may lead to undue haste and frustration. Be selective. Pace your teaching. Spend no more than five to ten minutes opening the lesson. During the lesson, get the sweep of meaning. Occasionally stop to help the class gain understanding of a word or concept. Allow approximately five minutes for closing the lesson and announcements.

Should your group have more than a one-hour class period, you can move at a more leisurely pace. But do not allow any lesson to drag and become tiresome. Keep it moving. Keep it alive. Keep it meaningful. Eliminate some questions and restrict yourself to those questions most meaningful to the members of the class. If most members study the text at home, they can report their findings, and the time gained can be applied to relating the lesson to life.

Good Preparation

Good preparation by you, the leader, usually affects the pleasure and satisfaction the class will experience.

Suggestions to the Leader for Using the Study Guide

The Lesson Pattern

This set of lessons is designed to aid *Bible study*, that is, to aid a consideration of the written Word of God, with discussion and personal application growing out of the text at hand.

The typical lesson is divided into these sections:

1. Theme verse
2. Objectives
3. Questions and answers
4. Closing

The theme verse and objectives give you assistance in arousing the group's interest in the concepts of the lesson. Here is where you stimulate minds of the class members. Do not linger too long over the introductory remarks.

The questions and answers provide the real spadework necessary for Bible study. Here the class digs, uncovers, and discovers; it gets the facts and observes them. Your comments are needed only to the extent that they help the group understand the text. The questions in this guide, corresponding to sections within the text, are intended to help the participants discover the meaning of the text.

Having determined what the text says, the class is ready to apply the message. Having heard, read, marked, and learned the Word of God, they can proceed to digest it inwardly through discussion, evaluation, and application. This is done, as these notes suggest, by taking the truths found in Scripture and applying them to the world and Christianity in general and then to one's personal Christian life. Class time may not permit discussion of all questions and topics. In preparation, you may need to select one or two and focus on them. Close the session by reviewing one important truth from the lesson.

Remember, the Word of God is sacred, but this study guide is not. The notes in this section offer only guidelines and suggestions. Do not hesitate to alter the guidelines or substitute others to meet your needs and the needs of the participants. Adapt your teaching plan to your class and your class period.

Good teaching directs the learner to discover for himself or herself. For you, the teacher, this means directing the learner, not giving the learner answers. Directing understanding takes preparation. Choose the verses that should be looked up in Scripture ahead of time. What discussion questions will you ask? At what points? Write them in the margin of your study guide. Involve class members, but give them clear directions. What practical actions might you propose for the week following the lesson? Which of the items do you consider most important for your class?

How will you best use your teaching period? Do you have forty-five minutes? an hour? an hour and a half? If time is short, what should you cut? Learn to become a wise steward of class time.

Plan a brief opening devotion, using members of the class. Be sure to take time to summarize the lesson or have a class member do it.

Remember to pray frequently for yourself and your class. May God the Holy Spirit bless your study and your leading of others into the comforting truths of God's Christ-centered Word.

Lesson 1

A Turning Point

Theme verse: *See, I have set the land before you. Go in and take possession of the land that the* L*ORD swore to your fathers, to Abraham, to Isaac, and to Jacob, to give to them and to their offspring after them.*

Deuteronomy 1:8

Objectives

By the power of the Holy Spirit working through God's Word, we will

- discover details of ancient treaties;
- learn of God's faithfulness to His people;
- see how man's sinfulness brings about God's reprimands, yet God's grace abounds.

Ancient Suzerain/Vassal Treaties

1. God uses devices humankind can understand. For example, using a suzerain/vassal treaty format with which His people were already familiar made it easier for them to remember His laws set before them.

2. Israel was about to begin its conquest of the Promised Land, a land God is giving them. Another "major turning point" comes with the leadership change about to occur. After forty years of leading God's people, Moses will soon hand over leadership to Joshua.

Preamble

3. The Israelites were encamped on the east side of the Jordan River. Using a Bible atlas, participants may note that this area is roughly opposite the city of Jericho, which is located at a distance on the western side of the river.

4. In the case of Israel, God allowed an entire unfaithful generation to die in the desert—raising up for Himself a new generation whom He would mold through Joshua. God may delay or even postpone events in our lives because we may not be prepared to handle them.

Historical Prologue

5. God had already fulfilled His promise to make Abraham's descendants "as numerous as the stars of heaven." Scholars estimate the number of Israelites ranged from one to two million people. The number of Israelites listed in Numbers 1:46 included only men over age twenty "able to go to war" and does not include women, those under twenty, or the infirm and those unable to go into battle.

6. Moses allowed each tribe to choose "wise, understanding, and experienced men" as leaders over them. Growing congregations should also appoint additional leaders to help guide them.

The Spies

7. By sending the spies into Canaan, the Israelites could check on the forces already in the land and receive a report about any of their weaknesses. God may have allowed the Israelites to send spies into Canaan in response to their weak faith in Moses' instructions to "Go up, take possession" of the land (v. 21).

8. In spite of God's Word, the Israelites did not believe God and rebelled against the idea of allowing Him to lead them into the Promised Land (vv. 32–33).

Rebellion against God

9. The strengthening of our faith is the work of God's Holy Spirit through the means of grace—God's Word and Sacraments.

10. God allowed Caleb and Joshua to enter the Promised Land while others of their generation passed away because of their rebellion.

By doing so, God demonstrated His grace by allowing experienced and faithful leaders to see them into the Promised Land.

Wandering

11. The time was right "as soon as all the men of war had perished." This marked the end of the generation age twenty and older at the time of the exodus.

12. At this time, Israel had no army, for "all the men of war had perished and were dead from among the people" (v. 16).

God's Word for Today

13. In our 1 Corinthians passage, Paul says that "God is faithful, and He will not let you be tempted beyond your ability." God knows our limits and provides means to stand up against the temptation to sin. Our source of strength is Jesus' sufferings, death, and resurrection for us, by which He conquered forever our sin.

14. Adam and Eve received God's first promise—that He would provide a Savior (Genesis 3:15). With each additional promise, God pointed forward to the coming of this Messiah, who would fulfill them. Jesus is the fulfillment of each and every promise made by God. Our faith truly rests in this knowledge.

Lesson 2

You Belong to God

Theme verse: *The LORD your God has given you this land to possess.*

Deuteronomy 3:18

Objectives

By the power of the Holy Spirit working through God's Word, we will

- learn of God's great victory over Israel's enemies;
- observe the planned division of the land by tribe;
- discover why God does not permit Moses to enter the Promised Land.

Setting the Stage

15. The Scriptures do not give us the exact reason why God chose this particular route. However, we do know that God guides and leads us through trials and tribulations in our lives in order that He might strengthen our faith and hope in Him (Romans 5:3–5).

16. Not only does God lead the Israelites, but He also cares for and protects other nations as evidenced by His protective hand over the Edomites, Moabites, and Ammonites. This is certainly an important point to consider when we consider world affairs—God is the Lord of all nations.

Defeat of Sihon

17. Because God desires the salvation of all (1 Timothy 2:3–4), He can use "terror and dread" to turn other nations to seek reconciliation with Israel and thus with Him. In this manner, foreign nations may come to know God and come to believe in the promised Messiah and be saved.

18. When people repeatedly spurn God's influence on their hearts, through His Word, God may harden them until they become calloused against the working of the Holy Spirit. In this case, a soul may be lost to eternity.

Defeat of Og

19. Answers will vary. God often strengthens our faith by using those around us. Moses often received God's reassurance during his travails—reassurance he passed on to his fellow Israelites.

20. When the spies arrived in Jericho, Rahab would report that hearts within the city were "melting" for fear of Israel.

Land Divisions

21. The three tribes requesting land east of the Jordan River included Gad, Reuben, and Manasseh. Moses stipulated that these three tribes provide military men who would fight beside their fellow tribesmen during the conquest of Canaan. These men could return home only at the completion of the conquest.

Moses Cannot Enter Canaan

22. God's anger burned against Moses because he had disobeyed Him. The precipitating event comes from Numbers 20:1–13. Note how Moses uses the word *we* in verse 10; in his anger, Moses essentially takes credit for a miracle God produced.

23. These words should reassure us that God does indeed love us, even as He disciplines us to strengthen our faith. When our faith is strengthened, the Holy Spirit can better use us to reach out as missionaries to those who do not believe in Jesus Christ as their Lord and Savior.

24. God appointed Joshua to succeed Moses. Because of his faith in God when the spies were first sent into Canaan, most would have felt Joshua was a good choice to succeed Moses.

25. Moses' responsibility toward Joshua included encouraging him and strengthening him. This Moses could accomplish by relating how God had provided for Moses during his years in God's service. We may still see examples of this strengthening and encouraging when an older pastor advises a younger pastor or when older members of a congregation advise younger members about how God has worked faith in their lives.

God's Word for Today

26. Without fear of reprisal, Moses could come before God and plead his case before Him. Moses' relationship with God allowed for times of disagreement, but ultimately, Moses surrendered his will to God's desires.

27. In the words of the Lord's Prayer, Jesus teaches us to call God "Father," indicating the intimate nature of our relationship with Him. Because our sins are forgiven in Jesus, we are restored to a right relationship with God.

Lesson 3

Set Apart by God

Theme verse: *To you it was shown, that you might know that the* LORD *is God; there is no other besides Him.*

Deuteronomy 4:35

Objectives

By the power of the Holy Spirit working through God's Word, we will

- discover Israel's uniqueness among the nations;
- learn that God does not take lightly the worship of other gods;
- observe God's mercy through the establishment of cities of refuge.

Setting the Stage

28. Answers will vary. We may avoid taking God for granted by staying in His Word through regular worship attendance, Bible study, and devotional time. We can also remember our Baptism daily with its drowning of the old Adam (Romans 6:3–8) and participate in Holy Communion.

29. Answers will vary. God has commanded the Church to tell others about Christ in the Great Commission (Matthew 28:19–20).

Baal-peor Reviewed

30. God saved those who "held fast to the Lord"; those who did not, perished.

31. Answers will vary. Sometimes "letting go of God" leads us farther from Him and deeper into sin. We give thanks that our God comes to us in our sin and leads us back to Himself through repentance and faith.

32. By observing God's laws and decrees, the Israelites provided a witness to God by their behavior. God desires that Christians show their love for God and one another through their deeds. These deeds do not earn salvation, but they do demonstrate a faith-filled life for all to see, as the Great Commission calls us to do.

No Idol Worship Allowed

33. The Canaanites worshiped pagan gods in the images of male and female human beings, animals, birds, creeping things, fish, the sun, moon, stars, and the hosts of heaven.

34. The "form" that God would eventually take is the God-man Jesus Christ, who is "the image of the invisible God" (Colossians 1:15).

35. Making graven images would provoke God's anger. Should the Israelites repent of following false gods, God would have mercy on them and remember His covenant with His people.

36. While God forbade the Israelites to create unauthorized images for use in divine worship, He did approve and command the use of some images. Cherubim made of hammered gold overlooked the mercy seat, the lid of the ark of the covenant upon which the high priest sprinkled blood on the Day of Atonement. Paul calls Jesus the mercy seat, or "propitiation" (in Greek, *hilasterion*), through the shedding of His blood (Romans 3:25). Likewise, cherubim were worked into the blue, purple, and scarlet curtain separating the Most Holy Place from the Holy Place. The writer to the Hebrews indicates that through Christ's blood and body ("the curtain"), we have immediate access to God (10:19–20). Jesus teaches that Moses' bronze serpent served as a type—that is, it pointed forward in time to Him and His sacrifice on the cross (John 3:14–15).

Cities of Refuge

37. With the establishment of cities of refuge, God protected those who accidentally killed another person. By fleeing to one of

these cities, one who had accidentally committed murder secured protection from those who sought to avenge the death.

God's Word for Today

38. Answers will vary. Sometimes we make idols of our possessions and our jobs. In so doing, we fail to recognize that the Lord has provided all that we have and that it is He alone whom we should worship.

39. God has had mercy on us and has forgiven us for the sake of the blood of His dear Son, Jesus Christ. For Christ's sake, we are spared the eternal damnation our sins merit, receiving instead the eternal life that Christ has merited on our behalf. Knowing that Christ has given His Church the keys to unlock heaven's mercy to us is a source of unending comfort and strength.

Lesson 4

God's Moral Law

Theme verse: *The LORD our God made a covenant with us in Horeb.*

Deuteronomy 5:2

Objectives

By the power of the Holy Spirit working through God's Word, we will

- grow to understand the covenant relationship God has with His people—then and now;
- discover the stipulations and commands of God's covenant with Israel, including details about the Ten Commandments;
- learn the importance of loving the Lord with your heart, soul and might.

"The Lord Spoke to You"

40. God is intimately involved with and concerned about His creation, especially His human creatures. He was with the Israelites in the cloud and provided passage through the sea; He gave them food to eat and water to drink. In each of these ways, God "saved" the Israelites. Paul will go on to say how Christ (the "rock" in the desert, 1 Corinthians 10:3) applies His saving work to us through the bread and wine at the Lord's Supper.

41. The spiritual missteps of our spiritual ancestors serve to warn us of the temporal consequences of our sins. Those who partake of the Lord's Supper unrepentantly, without faith in Christ, and without

discerning the Lord's body and blood in the Supper, do so to their own detriment (1 Corinthians 11:29–32).

An Introduction

42. While the word count following verse 44 is heavily weighted with Law verbiage, it is not without Gospel. In Deuteronomy 5, Moses reiterates the Ten Commandments, but not before reminding the Israelites that God had made a covenant with them (v. 2), and that it was this God who had saved them while they were held captive in Egypt (v. 6). When reading God's Law in these passages, we should always do so against the backdrop of the Gospel, that is, God's saving grace through Jesus Christ.

The Ten Commandments

43. The Ten Commandments, which are a restatement of God's moral law for the Israelites, nevertheless allow us to see our sins as if looking in a mirror. God's covenant and His work to bring about salvation for all people through His Son, Jesus Christ, abound even in the Book of Deuteronomy, which, at a cursory glance, appears only to provide rules and regulations to His peculiar people. The *torah*, however—the whole teaching of God, both Law and Gospel—should and must be taught to all new generations for the purpose of eliciting contrition and engendering faith.

44. God wants His people to "walk in all the ways the Lord [our] God has commanded [us]." We show our love for Him by keeping His commandments.

Love the Lord

45. Most participants should recognize the words "Hear, O Israel: The Lord our God, the Lord is one." Although prayed, the *Shema* is also a confession of faith in the unity of the Godhead.

46. By taking the Lord's grace for granted, we foster unbelief that manifests itself in further outward sin. Testing the Lord as His child merits His discipline. Doing so as an unbeliever merits His wrath.

47. We love God because He first loved us. We keep this command in loving response to what God has done through Christ.

God's Word for Today

48. We receive this great exchange—our sinful lives in exchange for Christ's sinless life—through faith that Jesus Christ died for our sins. Such faith is the work of the Holy Spirit working within us. It is a precious gift from God (Ephesians 2:8–9).

49. The two responses that Jesus mentions in this text are loving God and loving our fellowman.

Lesson 5

Only by God's Righteousness

Theme verse: *Know, therefore, that the LORD your God is not giving you this good land to possess because of your righteousness, for you are a stubborn people.*

Deuteronomy 9:6

Objectives

By the power of the Holy Spirit working through God's Word, we will

- acquaint ourselves with the pagan nations occupying the Promised Land;
- discover why God wanted these nations driven out of Canaan;
- learn that it is by God's righteousness that the Israelites come to live in the land promised to Abraham, Isaac, and Jacob.

A Who's Who in the Promised Land

50. God finds these practices detestable because they lead their practitioners away from Him to the worship of darkness and, eventually, to hell.

Drive Out the Canaanites

51. Moses told the Israelites that God would drive out the Canaanites from the Promised Land.

52. Yes, we often forget that God promises to be with us and never leave us. We should desire to remain connected to God through His Word and Sacraments.

53. These eight items were: to devote the Canaanites to complete destruction; not to make any agreements with them; to show them no mercy; not to intermarry with the Canaanites; to break down their altars; to dash their pillars into pieces; to chop down their Asherim poles (also centers of worship dedicated to the female goddess Asherath); and to burn their carved images.

54. Intermarriage with the Canaanites could cause the Israelites to lose their faith by worshiping false gods.

55. God promised to bless the wombs of the Israelite women and to bless the fruits of the fields—wine, grain, oil, and livestock. Note that God promised Israel abundant blessings if they would lovingly obey His ordinances.

56. The Israelites would have known that God fought their battles for them.

Remember God

57. God warns against taking credit for the power and might He has provided because such prideful boasting takes our eyes away from Him, our gracious giver God.

58. God warns that she would suffer the same consequences as the Canaanites if she should forsake Him and follow false gods.

God's Righteousness

59. Israel had no righteousness apart from God. We learn that God drove out the Canaanites not because of any righteousness Israel had, but because of the Canaanites' wickedness. Also, by driving the Canaanites out of the land, God kept His promises to Abraham, Isaac, and Jacob (Genesis 15:17–21; 26:3–6; 28:13–15).

The Golden Calf and Kadesh-barnea Remembered

60. Both times, Moses intervened before God on behalf of the Israelite nation. His prayers moved God to stay His hand of judgment. We see here the power of intercessory prayer.

God's Word for Today

61. The Holy Spirit intercedes on our behalf.

62. Answers will vary, but most should feel a reassurance that the Holy Spirit prays for us when our hearts are too heavy for words.

63. It is important to acknowledge that God saved us through Christ, for on our own, we have no righteousness to merit our salvation. Instead, we look to Christ who, from the cross, spoke the words "It is finished" (John 19:30), completing God's plan of salvation on our behalf.

Lesson 6

New Tablets

Theme verse: *And I will write on the tablets the words that were on the first tablets that you broke, and you shall put them in the ark.*

Deuteronomy 10:2

Objectives

By the power of the Holy Spirit working through God's Word, we will

- learn about the second giving of the Law and witness how God "keeps an eye on" His covenant;
- discover how God's grace was shown to His people;
- encounter the difference between a religion and a way of life.

Atonement through Christ

64. While the New Testament allows us to interpret the Old, studying the types and figures of Christ adds depth to our understanding of Christ and His work. The Yom Kippur (Day of Atonement) festival prefigures Christ in the work of the Jewish high priest, the shedding of blood, the forgiveness of sins, and so on.

65. Answers will vary. While the possibility of finding the true ark of the covenant may be remote (some believe it rests under the ancient Temple Mount or in Ethiopia), its rediscovery would serve to confirm the Christian faith. God, however, no longer directs our attention to the ark for His divine presence, but rather to our Savior, Jesus Christ, who is God in human flesh.

New Tablets

66. God was "keeping an eye" on the Ten Commandments contained in the ark, as well as the blood that was sprinkled on the lid of the ark for atonement.

67. Moses records the death and burial of his older brother, Aaron, the first high priest. Aaron's son Eleazar succeeded him.

68. The Lord said that He was the inheritance for the Levites. (For specifics on how God provided for His priests, see Leviticus 6:8–7:38.)

Fear the Lord

69. (a) verse 12a, (b) verse 12b, (c) verse 12c, (d) verse 12d, (e) verse 13

70. God gave this command to care for the sojourners (those who stayed in the land on a temporary basis) because at one time, Israel herself had been a sojourner in Egypt.

71. Yes, swearing by any other name is idolatry. While we may make oaths in God's name (Numbers 30:2; Deuteronomy 6:13; Hebrews 6:16), we should not do so lightly or with the intention of deceiving by God's name (Leviticus 19:12).

Love and Obey God

72. Canaan was different from Egypt in that God showered His blessings upon this land. He set this land apart as a prized possession for His people.

73. Should Israel depart from God's ways, God reserved the right to bring famine upon the land.

74. Although God's ways may seem harsh, He used famine to teach Israel the error of her ways and so that she might return to Him in repentant faith and enjoy His rich blessings.

75. God promised to drive the Canaanites out of the land. A standing army was not necessary, for God would fight Israel's battles. Our assurance comes from knowing that victory belongs to God even before the battle begins. As Christians, we take great joy in knowing that Christ has already won our battle over sin at the cross.

76. These permanent monuments throughout the land continually reminded Israel of what God had done on her behalf. Even with them, however, the memory of God's victories will fade.

God's Word for Today

77. Christians sometimes live no differently than their unchurched neighbors. Certainly, viewing Christianity as a way of life would make a difference in how we lived our lives. Instead of living for ourselves, we would live to serve others. Living in this manner would cause the world to take notice.

78. Through the Lord's Supper, God strengthens our faith and forgives our sins for the sake of Christ. Partaking of the Lord's Supper without repentance and faith may bring suffering and death, as it occurred among the Corinthians.

Lesson 7

God's Ceremonial Law

Theme verse: *But you shall seek the place that the* L*ORD* *your God will choose out of all your tribes to put His name and make His habitation there.*

Deuteronomy 12:5

Objectives

By the power of the Holy Spirit working through God's Word, we will

- examine the impossibility of sinners keeping God's Law and the assurance that Christ has kept them for us;
- explore God's command to establish one central place of worship with the rite of blood sacrifices foreshadowing Christ's sacrifice;
- discover God's call to beware of false prophets;
- learn how He provided for the well-being of His priests.

Fulfillment in Christ

79. All the Old Testament ceremonies and the laws that initiated them were fulfilled in Christ. Through faith in Him, we have the freedom to observe or not observe religious ceremonies—even Christian ones.

80. Answers will vary. The purpose of Christian ceremonies is to teach. Insofar as ceremonies point to Christ and can be observed without burdening consciences, they may be useful. Examples of such

ceremonies may be Christmas or Easter customs. Allow participants to name those ceremonies or traditions that are associated with these Christian holy days.

Holy Worship

81. The Israelites were forbidden to drink blood.

82. Leviticus 17:11 teaches us that God reserves the blood as an atonement for sins.

83. The shedding of blood is a foreshadowing of Christ's Good Friday sacrifice on the cross.

84. The Israelites will establish—at God's choosing—a central place for public worship. Centuries later, Jerusalem became the religious center of the Hebrew culture. The Israelites were commanded to destroy the Canaanite centers of pagan worship. God wanted to end the influence of these worship centers.

"False Prophets"

85. The Israelites were to ignore these individuals and remain faithful to God.

86. These individuals were to be "put to death" (v. 5).

87. Once a city's unfaithfulness was substantiated, the city was to be destroyed (vv. 12–16).

88. Yes, false prophets exist today. We see false prophets in any religion that draws Christians away from their belief in Jesus Christ as Lord and Savior. Jesus says that false prophets will perform miracles and that we should be wary of them.

89. Paul advised that Christians avoid false prophets, staying clear of their influences.

Clean and Unclean Food

90. With the exception of camels, hares, and rock badgers, animals that have a cloven hoof and chew their cud were judged "clean." Pigs have cloven hooves but do not chew their cud, so they were "unclean." Fish without scales were "unclean." Birds were "clean," except for those listed in verses 12–18. (Many of the birds listed there fit under the heading of scavengers.) Only those creatures that God designated as "clean" could be eaten or used for sacrifices.

Tithing

91. Our giving is an indicator of where our heart is. We should store up "treasures in heaven" through generous gifts of time, talent, and treasure for the Lord's work, rather than "treasures on earth." (See Matthew 6:19–20.)

92. The tithe of grain in the third year provided a source of food for the Levites, the fatherless, the widow, and the sojourner living in Israel. Answers to the second question will vary, but certainly, others could benefit from our gifts.

God's Word for Today

93. Christians may offer the "fruit of [their] lips" (v. 15) in praise for what God has done through the forgiveness of sins through Jesus Christ. Christians can also "do good" and "share what [they] have" (v. 16).

94. Answers will vary. We offer ourselves as living sacrifices by the way we live our lives. As situations arise, we might ask ourselves if others will see Christ by our actions. By caring for our fellow human beings, we live out our faith as God intends.

Lesson 8

Celebrating God's Grace

Theme verse: *Observe the month of Abib and keep the Passover to the LORD your God.*

Deuteronomy 16:1

Objectives

By the power of the Holy Spirit working through God's Word, we will

- learn how Israel remembered God's grace with feasts and celebrations;
- discover the ordinances governing the celebration of Passover;
- rejoice that Jesus Christ is the Passover Lamb who comes to us in Holy Communion for the forgiveness of our sins.

Christ, the True Redemption

95. By understanding the background of the initiation of the Passover, we see how God gave His Old Testament people a foretaste of the deliverance from sin fulfilled in Christ Jesus our Lord. Jesus is our "Passover lamb" (1 Corinthians 5:7).

96. Shared meals allow participants to bond. We see that in meals celebrated with friends and family as well as church potlucks. The Passover was more than just a fellowship meal, however, and Holy Communion is more than the Passover.

Cancelled Debts

97. We can imagine the broad appeal of a debt-cancellation festival. God wanted debts cancelled as a preview of the cancellation of the debt of sin that God accomplished through His precious Son. We see a simple restatement of this debt cancellation in the Lord's Prayer: "forgive us our sins, for we ourselves forgive everyone who is indebted to us" (Luke 11:4).

Servants Freed

98. An Israelite slave could serve for six years, but he or she was to be freed in the seventh year.

99. A freed slave could not be sent away empty-handed. Slaveholders were obligated to provide goods for freed slaves from their own livestock, grain, and winery. As God was generous to the slaveholder, so the slave owner was to be generous to the freed slave.

100. The Hebrews once had been enslaved to the Egyptians. By God's grace, they were granted their freedom. If the Israelites recalled this event, proper treatment of their fellowman should follow. Freeing their fellow Israelites would serve as a reminder of what God had done for them.

Firstborn Animals

101. God commanded that firstborn unblemished animals not be worked. Instead, they were sacrificed to God and their flesh eaten before God as a communal meal. The Israelites could not sacrifice blemished animals. They were free to eat those animals in their homes.

102. John records Jesus' words as "It is finished." We may also translate Christ's words as "It is paid for." Christ's atoning sacrifice through the shedding of His blood ransomed believers from eternal death.

Passover

103. Regulations governing the celebration of Passover include these: (a) sacrifice an animal from your flock in the city God selects as the worship center (v. 2); (b) eat unleavened bread for seven days (v. 3); (c) do not let any sacrificial meat remain until morning (v. 4); (d) do not offer your sacrifice in any town other than the one in which God

has chosen to dwell (vv. 5–6); (e) sacrifice in the evening of Passover at sunset (v. 6); (f) roast and eat the portion of meat in the town of God's choosing (v. 7); (g) return to your tents in the morning (v. 7); (h) on the seventh day, hold an assembly; in other words, come before God in worship (v. 8); (i) do not work (v. 8).

Feasts

104. The Feast of Weeks celebrates the Lord's blessing of a harvest. The Feast of Booths celebrates the end of the harvest season.

God's Word for Today

105. The two "memorials" instituted by Christ are Holy Baptism and the Lord's Supper.

106. In the communal meal of the Passover, the Israelites recalled the death of the lamb whose blood was placed on the door frames of their houses (Exodus 12:7) to protect them from death. So, too, we Christians recall the death of our Savior on the cross each time we celebrate the Lord's Supper (1 Corinthians 11:26). Just as the Israelites ate the sacrificial lamb, so, too, do we eat Christ's flesh and drink His blood (1 Corinthians 10:16), although in a spiritual or heavenly manner.

Lesson 9

God's Civil Laws

Theme verse: *The Levitical priests, all the tribe of Levi, shall have no portion or inheritance with Israel.*

Deuteronomy 18:1

Objectives

By the power of the Holy Spirit working through God's Word, we will

- see how God put in place a series of civil laws designed to govern His people;
- learn how judges and officers helped Moses govern the Israelites;
- discover how Jesus Christ fulfills God's plan for an earthly king.

A Solid Foundation

107. Answers will vary. The Israelites operated under a theocracy, a government based on religious laws. The legal system of the United States is based on the Constitution and other laws, which are themselves derived from natural law, the moral sense that, while marred by sin, remained in humankind after the fall. (See Romans 2:14–16.)

Judges and False Gods

108. Moses' requirements included that these judges be from among the tribes of Israel, that they not pervert justice, that they show no partiality, and that they accept no bribes.

109. Asherah poles and sacred stones represented the worship of false gods, which God did not permit. Since He alone rescued the Israelites from their enslavement in Egypt and He alone planned to fulfill His promises of land to the Israelites and a Savior for all humankind, God wants no rivals. He spells that out clearly in the Ten Commandments.

110. God wanted the evil "purged" before it could corrupt those who had faith. This statement regarding the purging of evil from Israel's midst showed God's love for them. God does not want anything standing in the way of His relationship with His people, thereby preventing them from spending eternity with Him.

111. Yes, the worship of false gods remains a problem today. False gods can be anything that takes our time or talents away from the worship of the God who created us, redeemed us, and sanctified us. Money, sports, people, and computer games—literally, anything that we value above the Lord God—can fall under the category "false gods."

Courts and Kings

112. The Levitical priests ruled in cases of homicides and assaults. The death penalty applied to individuals who rebelled against the rule of these men whom God had established to judge over them.

113. (a) verse 15a, (b) verse 15b, (c) verse 16a, (d) verse 16b, (e) verse 17a, (f) verse 17b, (g) verse 18, (h) verse 19

114. King David and King Solomon might well have come to mind. God placed these restrictions on His kings so that they would remain faithful to Him and not rely on their own abilities.

Priestly and Levitical Offerings

115. God provided for His priests and Levites through the offerings of His people. These men received the shoulder, cheeks, and stomach of each sacrifice, as well as the firstfruits of grain, wine, and oil, and the first fleece of their sheep. Should a Levite visit a town, the Israelites there were to provide him food.

Deplorable Practices

116. The deplorable practices include (a) the burning of one's child as an offering; (b) the practice of divination; (c) telling fortunes; (d) interpreting omens; (e) being a sorcerer; (f) being a charmer; (g) being a medium; (h) being a necromancer (one who conjures spirits of the dead). All of these practices indicate the worship of gods apart from the one true God.

117. Several deplorable practices continue, such as divination, fortune-telling, interpreting omens, sorcery, and being a medium and a necromancer. Tragically, some Christians think nothing of consulting a fortune-teller, participating in occult practices such as using a Ouija board, or reading their daily horoscope. We should avoid and repent of these sins.

God's Word for Today

118. Christ came to serve (Mark 10:45). A godly king should serve his people. The second kingly characteristic of Christ is that He heeded God's voice alone (John 5:30). A godly king should follow God's rule for his life. In addition, Jesus Christ came into the world to give His life for His people (1 Timothy 1:15). A godly king should be willing to give up his life for his people.

119. A servant king willingly lays down his power and authority to serve the needs of his people. Although Jesus Christ is true God, He became true man for us so that He might save us from our sin by His sinless, obedient life and His atoning death. God's words in Deuteronomy point forward to the time of Christ—God's Servant King.

Lesson 10

More Civil Laws

Theme verse: *The* L*ORD your God will raise up for you a prophet like me from among you, from your brothers—it is to Him you shall listen.*

Deuteronomy 18:15

Objectives

By the power of the Holy Spirit working through God's Word, we will

- learn how Moses' words of a coming Prophet point to Jesus Christ;
- discover additional civil laws that apply to cities of refuge, preparations for war, and unsolved murders;
- rejoice that although we cannot keep God's Law, Jesus Christ did on our behalf.

A Man Hung on a Tree

120. Answers will vary. Allow participants to share as much of their personal experiences as they want. Usually, it is only after we've undergone our cross (curse) that we can see and appreciate God's hand of blessing in the midst of our difficulties.

The Prophet

121. These distinguishing features reveal that this Prophet not only comes from God, but is God Himself.

122. Allow participants to share their opinions. False prophets continue to exist. We may apply the same measuring stick: a prophet who speaks for God must speak God's Word.

Cities of Refuge

123. Cities of refuge placed at regular intervals allowed those falsely accused of murder to reach safety no matter what direction they fled for protection. God protected the falsely accused and those who killed by accident from death at the hands of an avenger.

124. The accidental murderer lived, while the premeditated murderer received the death penalty.

125. Ultimately, God exacts justice through the government.

126. The elders were required to hand over the murderer to the avenger in order that the murderer could be executed.

Preparations for War

127. Like a loving Father, God offered reassurance to Israel that He would be with them in their battles against the Canaanites.

128. God fights this battle for us and with us. We have Jesus' words to accompany us and reassure us: "And behold, I am with you always, to the end of the age" (Matthew 28:20).

Unsolved Murder and Other Provisions

129. We can apply the word *kaphar* ("to cover") to the work of Christ. Indeed, in His death, God covered our sin so that whenever God looks upon us, He does so through the redeeming blood of His Son, Jesus Christ. Therefore, instead of seeing our unrighteousness, He sees Christ's righteousness imputed to us.

God's Word for Today

130. Answers will vary. We should all feel humbled that the same God who created the universe, the earth, and all that is in it sent His own Son to die in our stead. He alone kept all of God's laws perfectly for us. This fact is worth sharing with others.

Lesson 11

Follow the Lord

Theme verse: *This day the LORD your God commands you to do these statutes and rules.*

Deuteronomy 26:16

Objectives

By the power of the Holy Spirit working through God's Word, we will

- familiarize ourselves with God's laws against sexual immorality;
- learn about laws governing the Israelite encampment;
- discover that through Christ, God has made a new covenant with the world—one that involves His atoning death for all humankind.

God, the Protector of Life

131. Love always involves putting the interests of others ahead of our own. Love doesn't seek its own good; it seeks that of others. God loves His creation, especially His human creatures, and is intimately concerned and active in their lives—down to their very breath.

132. Often how we treat animals reflects our attitude toward life. Proverbs 12:10 echoes this same thought: "Whoever is righteous has regard for the life of his beast, but the mercy of the wicked is cruel."

Sexual Immorality

133. The man who falsely accused his wife of infidelity before their marriage received a whipping and a fine of a hundred shekels of silver. In addition, he could never divorce his wife. If the man's accusations proved true and his wife had had premarital sex, she was stoned in front of her father's house.

134. **verse 22:** If a man slept with another man's wife, both were to be put to death.

verses 23–24: If a betrothed woman lay with a man within the city gates, both were put to death outside the city gate.

verses 25–27: If a man raped a woman outside the city gate, he alone would die.

verses 28–29: If a man raped a virgin, he had to pay her father fifty shekels and he could never divorce her.

verse 30: A man could not have sex with his father's wife. (Scholars tell us that this woman was not the man's mother, but his stepmother. Regardless, the man was forbidden to have sex with her.)

God takes very seriously the relationship between a man and his wife and does not permit anything to stand in the way of the marital relationship He has instituted. Sex outside of marriage does not fit into God's plan.

135. This sentence comes as a restatement of an earlier passage describing God's abhorrence of sin. God will not associate with sin because of His holy nature. God's intolerance of sin has not changed, for He remains the same yesterday, today and tomorrow (Hebrews 13:8).

Laws for Assembly and Camp

136. God excluded men with crushed sexual organs and those born of a forbidden relationship. This involved children born in relationships between Canaanites and Hebrews. God excluded the Ammonites and Moabites from assembling with the Jews because they did not greet their relatives with food when they came to them and because they hired Balaam to curse them. God did not exclude the Edomites because of their relationship to the Israelites through Lot; He did not exclude the Egyptians because the Israelites had sojourned in Egypt.

Other Laws

137. By making divorces so difficult to obtain, God hoped to limit their number and the problems and heartaches divorces can cause.

138. In a Levirate marriage, a woman whose husband died could expect her husband's brother to marry her in hope of producing a son to care for her in her old age. God permitted such marriages to allow the perpetuation of family names.

139. God forbade the carrying of two different weights while traveling or at home. By having only one weight, the Israelites again set themselves apart from the nations around them. God promised long days in their new homeland for treating each other fairly.

Firstfruits and Tithes

140. Humankind's forgetfulness plays an important role in God's desire that the Israelites not forget His gracious deeds on their behalf.

141. Christ commanded us to remember Him each time we partake of Holy Communion. By remembering Him, we recall what He did on the cross and take to heart the real presence of His body and blood in, with, and under the bread and wine.

142. Each time we receive Communion, we should remember His sacrifice for the forgiveness of our sins.

Admonishments

143. Israel agreed to "walk in [God's] ways, and keep His statutes and His commandments and rules" (Deuteronomy 26:17). God agreed to treasure His people and "set [them] in praise and in fame and in honor high above all nations" (vv. 18–19).

144. Often we may consider others worthless. However, in God's eyes, all are "treasured possessions."

God's Word for Today

145. God sealed this new covenant in the blood of His Son, Jesus Christ.

146. Like God's Old Testament people, we may say to God, "What have you done for me lately?" Instead, we should remember that the greatest blessing God can bestow on us, the forgiveness of sins, was won for us at a terrible price: the death of God's Son.

Lesson 12

God's Covenant Ratified

Theme verse: *Keep silence and hear, O Israel: this day you have become the people of the* LORD *your God.*

Deuteronomy 27:9

Objectives

By the power of the Holy Spirit working through God's Word, we will

- learn about the blessings and curses that accompany God's covenant with Israel;
- rejoice in the grace that God promised even when Israel fell away from Him;
- discover more about God's amazing plan of salvation through Jesus Christ.

Twin Peaks

147. The two chief teachings of Scripture that stand over our lives like Mount Gerizim and Mount Ebal are Law and Gospel.

148. Answers will vary. In such instances, some participants may feel that something had been lacking in worship.

149. John wrote, "If we say we have no sin, we deceive ourselves, and the truth is not in us. If we confess our sins, He is faithful and just to forgive us our sins and to cleanse us from all unrighteousness" (1 John 1:8–9). Confessing our sin—whether privately, to another individual, or in public worship—and receiving

God's absolution through the Gospel are part and parcel of the Christian life.

Mount Ebal

150. The descendants of the tribes of Simeon, Levi, Judah, Issachar, Joseph, and Benjamin offered the blessings from Mount Gerizim, while the descendants of the tribes of Reuben, Gad, Asher, Zebulun, Dan, and Naphtali offered the curses from Mount Ebal.

151. (a) verse 15, (b) verse 16, (c) verse 17, (d) verse 18, (e) verse 19, (f) verse 20, (g) verse 21, (h) verse 22, (i) verse 23, (j) verse 24, (k) verse 25, (l) verse 26

Mount Gerizim

152. **verse 1:** God will set Israel over all other nations.

verse 3: God will bless cities and fields.

verse 4: God will bless the fruit of the womb, the harvests, and the livestock.

verse 5: God will bless all household endeavors.

verse 6: God will bless all everyday activities.

verse 7: God will defeat Israel's enemies.

verse 8: God will bless Israel's barns as well as everything the people undertake.

verse 9: God will make Israel holy.

verse 10: All nations will fear the nation of Israel.

verse 11: God will make Israel prosperous.

verse 12: God will bring rainfall in its season. Israel will loan but never borrow, showing how abundantly God has blessed her.

verse 13: God will supply Israel with everything she needs. She will lead and not follow; she will progress and not decline.

More Curses

153. Should Israel disobey God, God would allow a "hard-faced nation" (Deuteronomy 28:50) to drive Israel from her land (v. 64). Israel's land promise remained in effect so long as she followed God. She could negate this portion of her covenant with God by following the religious practices of the Canaanites—and she would. Israel would

pay for this disobedience by being taken captive by the Assyrians and the Babylonians. By God's grace, the most important part of His covenant, the promise of a Savior, is irrevocable. This promise is not contingent upon Israel's faithfulness.

Renewal

154. Those nations that see Israel taken into captivity would realize that her downfall came because she had broken her covenant with God by serving other gods. God will use Israel's captivity to witness to other nations who observe Israel's struggles.

Life or Death

155. God graciously offers forgiveness and restoration after Israel realizes her error and returns to Him in worship.

156. God will send His Holy Spirit to strengthen the hearts of believers who return to Him. Anyone who persecutes those returning to Him shall be cursed, while those who return shall receive His blessing.

157. Believing in God for the forgiveness of sins through Christ brings with it eternal life; without this belief, only eternal death exists.

God's Word for Today

158. Peter's beautiful confession captures the essence of true belief in Christ: Lord, where else can we turn? You have the words of eternal life.

Lesson 13

Succession of Leadership

Theme verse: *Call Joshua and present yourselves in the tent of meeting, that I may commission him.*

Deuteronomy 31:14

Objectives

By the power of the Holy Spirit working through God's Word, we will

- understand what it means to follow God's will, not our own;
- see how God provided a successor for Moses;
- thank God for the life of Moses, who pointed forward to the time of Christ—our true deliverer.

God's Will—Is It Our Desire?

159. Answers will vary. Our sinful natures want to grasp and control the direction of our lives. Surrendering control often proves too hard, although we pray that God's will be done each time we pray the Lord's Prayer. Ultimately, we must cling to God's gracious promises in His Word, including the promise that He works all things for our good (Romans 8:28).

Joshua

160. Had we been in Joshua's sandals, we would have been encouraged by knowing that God goes before us and that He will not leave or forsake us. These same words apply to us as we consider

letting go of the micromanagement of our lives and surrendering everything into the Lord's hands.

161. After he had written down all the Lord had dictated to him (Deuteronomy 31:9), Moses entrusted Israel's copy of God's laws to the priests and elders.

162. Through Moses, God commanded the Israelites to hear His laws read every seven years.

Rebellion Foretold

163. Answers will vary. We may find it hard to imagine that God loves us even though He knows our thoughts and actions before they occur. How thankful we are that He foreknew our need for a Savior and provided "Christ Jesus before the ages began" (2 Timothy 1:9).

Song of Moses

164. Answers will vary. Discussion might center on the unchangeable nature of a rock. Think of the Rock of Gibraltar, and talk about how it symbolizes stability. Our God is steadfast and immovable in His love of sinners.

165. The list of kindnesses appears in Deuteronomy 32:7–14. The Song of Moses reveals many examples of God's kindness toward His people. For example, God "gave to the nations their inheritance" and "fixed the borders of the peoples according to the number of the sons of God" (v. 8). It also includes a dramatic retelling of how God cared for the Israelites during their forty years of wandering.

166. God did not want His enemies to gloat by thinking that by their own powers, they had won victory over God's people.

Last Days of Moses

167. Moses died on Mount Nebo, and God personally buried him.

God's Word for Today

168. Moses' life pointed forward in anticipation of the coming of Jesus Christ, an even greater prophet and deliverer. Through Christ, we have been delivered from our sins and the punishment they deserve, we have been adopted into God's family, and we will enjoy eternal life.

We give thanks for faithful servants like Moses, whose words and deeds led others to the Servant of servants, Jesus Christ.

169. The real hero of Deuteronomy is God. He alone led His people to the east side of the Jordan. By God's hand, Moses instructed God's people about how to live in harmony with Him and with one another. God constantly instructed, warned, and disciplined His people. God called His people to Himself even when they distrusted Him, and He fulfilled all of His promises to them through Christ.

170. Answers will vary. We should find ourselves awe-filled, knowing that we worship the same God that Moses did. While Moses waited for the coming of Jesus Christ and the forgiveness of sins He would bring, we rejoice that Jesus has come and fulfilled all the promises God made (2 Corinthians 1:20).